Female Improvisational Poets: Challenges and Achievements in the Twentieth Century

D1365394

Center for Basque Studies
University of Nevada, Reno

Female Improvisational Poets: Challenges and Achievements in the Twentieth Century

Editors:
Xabier Irujo and Iñaki Arrieta

Center for Basque Studies
University of Nevada, Reno
Reno, Nevada 89557
http://basque.unr.edu

ISBN-13: 978-1-949805-04-8
ISBN-10: 1-949805-04-2

Conference Papers Series No. 15
Series Editor:
Sandra Ott

Center for Basque Studies
University of Nevada, Reno
Reno, Nevada 89557
http://basque.unr.edu

Contents

Female Improvisational Poets: Challenges and Achievements in the Twentieth Century

Xabier Irujo and Iñaki Arrieta Baro

On December 13, 2009, 14,500 people met at the Bilbao Exhibition Centre in the Basque Country to attend an improvised poetry contest. It was the fifteenth edition of this particular Basque national poetry gathering. Forty-four poets took part in the 2009 literary tournament, and eight of them made it to the final. After a long day of literary competition, Maialen Lujanbio won and received the award: a big black *txapela* or Basque beret.

That day the Basques achieved a triple triumph. First, thousands of people had gathered for an entire day to follow a literary contest, and many more had attended the event via the web or on TV and the radio, all over the world. Second, all these people had followed this event entirely in Basque, a language that had been prohibited for decades during the harsh years of the Francoist dictatorship and that, according to the data provided by the UNESCO, in the late 1970s was on the brink of extinction. And third, Lujanbio had become the first woman to win the championship in the history of the Basques.

After being crowned with the *txapela*, Lujanbio stepped up to the microphone and sung a *bertso* or improvised poem referring to the struggle of the Basques for their language and the struggle of Basque women for their rights. It was a unique moment in the history of an ancient nation that counts its past in tens of millennia:

Gogoratzen naiz lehengo amonen	I remember the laundry that grandmothers
zapi gaineko gobaraz	of earlier times carried on the cushion [on their heads]
gogoratzen naiz lehengo amonaz	I remember the grandmother of old times
gaurko amaz ta alabaz. . . .	and today's mothers and daughters. . . .
Gure bidea ez da errexa	Our journey is not an easy one
bete legez, juizioz, trabas...	Full of laws, court cases, obstacles,
Euskal Herriko lau ertzetara	we shall return to the four corners
itzuliko gara gabaz	the Basque Country at night,
Eta hemen bildu dan indarraz	And with the strength that we have harvested here,
grinaz eta poz taupadaz	with passion and heartbeats of joy,
herri hau sortzen segi dezagun	let's continue building this country
euskaratik ta euskaraz.	from and with the Basque language.

A big ovation followed her voice.

Bertsolaritza or Basque improvisational poetry is the art of voicing the moment.[1] A *bertso* is an improvised verse as opposed to an *olerki*, which is a written poem. The *bertsoak* are composed on the spot. The poet is often given the theme or the rhythm or the meter or all of them together by the moderator, and then the poet must start singing according to what she or he has been given. Sometimes the poet is given words that have to rhyme, and he or she must work with them. There are often contests between two or three (or many more) *bertsolariak* or singing poets, so they have to defend an idea: for instance, a young woman in love who has to convince a beautiful partner to kiss her while the other *bertsolari* counters her desires. Often, however, there are also sad, satirical, political, and profoundly philosophical *bertsoak* as well. There are city, regional, and national level bertso contests. The first bertsoak to be published in Basque appeared in 1545, and some of the melodies can date back half a millennium.[2]

The present book will address the struggle for the rights of women in the context of bertsolaritza (improvised oral poetry) in the Basque Country. It is a good case study since the critical situation and development of the Basque language and Basque culture has historically conditioned the state of bertsolaritza and continues to do so today. At the same time, it is also an excellent case study to analyze the struggle for the rights of women in the context of a minority culture that battles for its own cultural survival.

The book opens with the chapter by Jone Miren Hernandez' "I See a Body in Your Voice: Gendered Bodies in the Sound of Bertsolaritza," which contemplates a historical journey with the aim of examining more closely the growing social importance that bertsolaritza has acquired through the years, paying particular attention to its development since the 1930s. Hernandez underlines the close ties between bertsolaritza and society, the qualitative space

---

1 Samuel G. Armistead and Joseba Zulaika, eds., *Voicing the Moment: Improvised Oral Poetry and Basque Tradition*, (Reno: Center for Basque Studies Press, University of Nevada, Reno, 2003).

2 Xabier Irujo, "Bertso," *World Literature Today* (September–October 2007), 44–45.

created by bertsolaritza and especially the National Bertsolaritza Championship, the importance of this for creating and recreating (Basque) culture, and, finally, the participation of women bertsolaris in the feminist movement.

Hernandez places the participation of women bertsolariak in the context of contemporary bertsolaritza. The trajectory of women bertsolaris may be summarized in three stages: (1) the "emergence" of women bertsolaris (in the 1980s and 1990s), (2) the preoccupations and demands of women bertsolaris in search of their own identity and voice (the period between 2000 and 2010), and (3) the situation today: that created by the appearance of feminism on the stage, both within bertsolaritza itself but also among the audience and society as a whole.

Bertsolaritza has traditionally depicted society by improvising on actual, problematic topics. The creation topic could be given by the theme-prompter or chosen freely by the improvisers. Bertsolariak performing publicly have been traditionally men, and therefore, female characters have been performed by men until the first women came on stage. Women brought some changes to the discourse about social issues and to the depiction of roles. Based on those changes, Oihana Iguaran in her chapter "Women in Bertsogintza: From Being a Subject to Being Capable" answers two main questions: 1) How female voices were performed during the last thirty years and 2) How the inclusion of women affected the performed roles. The first findings show that female characters used to be related to male ones and less shaped than the others (for example, just introduced as moms, wives, daughters). The number of female roles has turned around, not for the amount of male roles but for the many themes that do not specify the sex of the characters. Another evolution of female roles is that thirty years ago female ones used to be referred to, not referring. Nowadays regular performances usually have one or two women at least. Despite in championship the themes are decided by lottery, in other performances being a woman determines many times what they are singing about. The ongoing change brought by women helps to understand how diversity widens the representation of society, which could be applied to many other social groups.

According to Maialen Lujanbio, bertsolaritza is by definition a contemporary activity since the poet's purpose is always to sing in his or her own surroundings. However, this environment in which the bertsolari sings has changed drastically in the last thirty years. Along with this social change, the bertsolariak have also changed. In her chapter "As the Tree Grows, the Bark Cracks," Lujanbio analyzes what has been referred to as a critical factor for the modernization of bertsolaritza that began in the 1980s: the creation of bertso-eskolak or bertso schools. For the first time boys and girls could learn bertsolaritza together at these bertso-eskolak, and later they all gathered to sing along in squares all over the country. An increasingly younger generation of bertsolariak attracted an also younger public to the streets and this way the movement that reformed bertsolaritza started with its different thematic, aesthetic, and corporal profiles. The study of the last thirty years of the history of bertsolaritza provides significant clues about contemporary creative practices and helps to shape the direction in which bertsolaritza is to be developed in the future.

In "Contemporary Women Bertsolaris: The Tale of a Possible Empowerment Process," Miren Artetxe analyzes the changes that the Basque improvised poetry has demonstrated since women began to practice it. Indeed, the rise of women to bertsolaritza was a factor of evolution. During the last decade, the number of women bertsolariak has increased both in the squares and in the championships. The transformation goes beyond participation: the practice of bertsolaritza has generated new shared spaces, the vision of bertsolaritza from the perspective of feminism has changed, and the means to open bertsolaritza up to women bertsolariak have been increased.

However, there is a danger in the transformation of social or cultural movements. On the one hand, we could understand empowerment as an extra-structural element, understanding the process of empowerment as a means to promote self-esteem and strengthen individual power. From this perspective, by observing the process of empowerment, it is possible to describe the intrinsic value of interacting with structural power relations. Miren Artetxe's chapter analyses the transformation of women into a feminist bertsolaritza toward the transformation of women of bertsolaritza, based on her own experience as a bertsolari, as well as in the conversations she has had with other bertsolariak.

Larraitz Ariznabarreta, in her chapter "The Presence of Women Bertsolaris as a Kind of Historical Comeback" also refers to the evolution of Basque improvisational poetry. In her view, bertsolaritza is becoming one of the most gripping subject matters of the last decade, assigning it a relationship with everything and anything in whichever manner and field. According to the author, a circle has been closed: traditional canonical poets turned out to be aloof to grassroots people, and bertsolariak strove to "poeticize" the old Basque intelligentsia; whereas new bertsolaritza has put the very academy itself at its service, with the conviction that it is the only way and the least exhausting method to endow it with a Basque culture label. As gender discourse goes beyond women's presence and demand for equal opportunities, the ambiguity of gender and sex-role are subjects of discussion onstage.

In "What is the Sex of a Bertsolaria?" Joseba Zulaika discusses the bertsolaritza art's impasses and breakthroughs—most relevantly in relation to gender. In literature, there is the emblematic deadlock in which Beckett found himself and which led him to write *Texts for Nothing*. While frequently placed in competitive contexts to win the *txapela*, Zulaika asks in which way the bertsolaria must feel defeated in the imaginative risks that he or she takes, aware that defeat is the inevitable result of artistic creation. In particular, he wonders what the implications of singing are in a post-patriarchal Basque society in which women no longer function as idealized substitutes for male projections but as real bodies who sing side by side with men. The links between competitive *joko* games and men's spheres in traditional culture are drawn; leaving aside the fantasy of winning, cases of deliberate self-sabotage by bertsolariak are also discussed. Finally, the chapter calls for a transition from Lekuona's theoretical work to a contemporary feminist theory regarding bertsolaritza; it emphasizes the need to interlink domains of body experience and areas of knowledge in the formation of new subjectivation processes.

The book ends with two references to the women's struggle in the universe of Western American literature as a way to contrast that with what has happened in the Basque Country. Carolyn Dufurrena, in her chapter "Basque and Buckaroo: Women at Work in the Nevada Desert," discusses how in the last three decades Western women poets and writers have been given a nationally recognized platform. The Western Folklife Center has made it possible to present ranching culture and ranching stories from a woman's perspective to a wide audience through the National Cowboy Poetry Gathering.

As a consequence, rural western society defines the artists by the work they do. The author asks: Who are ranch women? Cooks? Gardeners? Schoolteachers? Cowboys? Women who rope and ride in the course of their daily lives, who see the ranching culture from their own unique perspective, now have a place to share their stories, their poems, and songs. They tell the stories of each other, their relationships; the calves they save, the horses they ride, the floods and fires and droughts through which they live. It is a world seen through the feminine lens, a different perspective on life in the West.

The book finishes with Amy Hale Auker's chapter "Work Song: A Female Voice from Cow Camp." In *If Women Rose Rooted*, Sharon Blackie says that the feminine voice and the feminine story will save our planet. As female voices continue to emerge and strengthen, the stories from women in agriculture, those growing food, may be some of the sweetest. The author finds that in her own writing, her voice is sometimes strident, sometimes soft, as she falls further in love with the land, learning how to do a job that is traditionally done by men. And yet, women are intrinsically equipped to be herders of mammals. As Auker sees it, "we ovulate, copulate, gestate miracles in our bodies, and lactate for months. While my job may demand that I am tough physically, when I lie down at night, I am richer for having seen the land and the animals as only a woman can, from the smallest earthworm to the bear that crossed my path in the canyon. And my voice speaks for more than my gender."

The Center for Basque Studies and the Basque Library participated in the Thirty-Fourth National Cowboy Poetry Gathering held annually in Elko, Nevada by organizing the Fifteenth Annual Basque

Conference and several cultural activities in the context of what ended up being a fourteen-day week. As noted on the blog of the Center for Basque Studies, the 2018 Elko festival (January 29–February 4) was thus focused on "the contributions of Basques in the West and included sessions on Basque arborglyphs, Basque poetry, Basque writing, the experience of Basques in ranching—featuring the insight of longtime Nevada resident and stalwart of Winnemucca's Basque community, Frank Bidart—only 95 years young!"[3]

As Lujanbio said to Suzanne Featherston, a reporter on the *Elko Daily*, "Bertsolaritza is a traditional but contemporary art, and I think it is one of the most powerful meeting points for Basque speakers. We hope to show our way of singing, our improvising tradition and above all our language. The Basque language is alive and is our main tool to create our poetry, in which we express our opinions, feelings and our point of view towards any current affairs."[4] She was not mistaken: barely a month after she won the *txapela* for the second time in the National Bertsolaritza Competition celebrated in the Basque Country in December 2017, nine hundred English-speaking cowboys and cowgirls gathered to listen to the five Basque bertsolariak improvising poetry in Basque on a cold winter night at the Elko Convention Center in Nevada. Next, whether wearing berets or cowboy hats, they all went together for a drink to the rhythm of Caitlin Belem's fiddle.

---

3   "Basque culture, Basque books, and bertsoak bloom in Elko at the National Cowboy Poetry Gathering," Basque Blog of the Center for Basque Studies, February 8, 2018, at https://basquebooks.blogs.unr.edu/basque-culture-basque-books-and-bertsoak-bloom-in-elko-at-the-national-cowboy-poetry-gathering/.

4   "Champion bertsolari to perform improvised Basque verse at gathering," *Elko Daily*, January 28, 2018. http://elkodaily.com/entertainment/champion-bertsolari-to-perform-improvised-basque-verse-at-gathering/article_9de92233-872a-51bc-b701-eb237c7705bf.html.

Bibliography

Armistead, Samuel G., and Joseba Zulaika, eds. *Voicing the Moment: Improvised Oral Poetry and Basque Tradition.* Reno: Center for Basque Studies Press, University of Nevada, Reno, 2003.

Irujo, Xabier. "Bertso." *World Literature Today* (September–October 2007): 44–45.

CHAPTER 1

I See a Body in Your Voice: Gendered Bodies in the Sound of Bertsolaritza

Jone M. Hernández García

When I was young, at school,[1] there was a typical punishment handed out on any given day if you did something *bad*, namely being obliged to summarize what you had done in a sentence and writing that out multiple times. The punishment could have been for a variety of reasons, not doing your homework for example or because you had caused some disturbance in class. Yet, among many others, one sentence was especially unforgettable: "I will not speak in class again. I will not speak in class again. I will not speak in class again…" Pages and pages were filled with that sentence, handwritten with a ballpoint pen, seeking to correct a behavior, in silence, and seeking to embody silence.

---

1   In this case, when I say school, I am talking about school in the early 1970s. I am talking about the public school system under the control of the Franco regime.

We find the materiality of the body by word of mouth, in voice, sound. Voice is no more than a body (Ferrete, quoted in Villaverde 2016, 3). For example, the teachers back then were so wise that, with the aim of controlling and disciplining the voice, they punished the body, causing cramp in the children's hands or just major boredom.

Releasing voice from bodies fulfills a context, creating all kinds of consequences: happiness (when a friend greets us), annoyance (when we are startled by a shout), anger (when we hear something cruel), a laugh (when something touches our emotions), and so on. I believe that the voice itself and what the voice implies are necessary in order to situate oneself in reality and to maintain reality. The voice is a support, whether individual or collective, created by creatures and humans, produced and extended in order to get in touch with a context and to get closer to that context itself. By way of one clear example, half-jokingly half-seriously, like when we try and create and echo. Yet even in a less explicit way, all voices and sounds seek or need that round trip: we want influence in the world (through voice), in order to be able to feel part of the world in return.

With these considerations serving as a stimulus, this chapter will discuss the role of voice in bertsolaritza, highlighting the influence of voice in the *modernization* of bertsolaritza. At the same time, it will discuss the extent to which women bertsolari's participation has conditioned the importance modern bertsolaritza has given to voice. And in that same vein, lastly, there will be a consideration of the possible contribution that the development of feminist bertsolaritza has had on voice as a tool of gender differentiation.

In order to develop and structure this reflection, I will incorporate several theoretical approaches from social anthropology as well as several ethnographical examples taken from throughout the 2017 National Bertsolaritza Championship of the Basque Country, focusing on the voice of the bertsolari Maialen Lujanbio. Lujanbio was the 2017 champion, performing some of the most amazing bertsos ever heard at the championship, in public. In order to understand the influence of those bertsos I think that we need to turn to the anthropology of affect (Surralles 1998, 2009a, 2009b; Hernández 2016, 2017). That is, an anthropology that surpasses and/or will include the rhetorical and discursive elements found in a bertso. This text takes that approach, offering complementary elements and perspectives in understanding and defining bertsolaritza.

Bertsolari, Bertso, Bertsolaritza: What are We Talking About?

Any definition of the words "bertsolari," "bertso," and/or "bertsolaritza" is closely linked to time and place, that is, naturally, their nature and features have changed a lot over time and according to the context. Manuel Lekuona (1978) says that it is a tradition dating from the Neolithic and, specifically, that it came from "within the shepherding tradition" (ibid., 12). At a certain point Basque lifestyles shifted from shepherding to agriculture and, then, according to Lekuona, "bertsolaritza expanded into the agricultural lifestyle too. Into the agricultural and manufacturing lifestyle" (ibid., 15).

As regards ancient bertsolaritza, we only have hypotheses and speculations. Joxe Azurmendi (1980, 1990) has also raised several doubts in his reflection on the beginnings and historical development of that tradition, emphasizing the gray areas bertsolaritza raises. Azurmendi contends that two forces have collided in the realm of bertsolaritza (Azurmendi 1980, 143): first, one that has made an overly easy myth of the ancient nature of bertsolaritza. And second, the anti-myth, in other words one that claims that bertsolaritza is a completely modern phenomenon in the Basque Country (created in the nineteenth century).

While we do have references to some concept of bertsolari, bertso, and/or bertsolaritza in the fifteenth century, similar references have only been considered worthy of study when dating from the eighteenth, nineteenth, and especially twentieth centuries: "It could be said, then, that until the twentieth century we have had no way of studying the improvised corpus" (Garzia, Sarasua, and Egaña 2001, 20). Indeed, there was a major obstacle to transforming bertsolaritza into a topic of study: with no means of remaining in the memory of listeners, bertsos were scattered to the wind. For that reason, researchers especially appreciate the first bertso corpus made up of *bertso-paperak* or *bertso-jarriak* (bertsos printed on paper) in the nineteenth and twentieth centuries.

Beyond this obstacle being the chief consequence of having such few resources for researchers and the intellectual-academic world in general to reflect on bertsolaritza, Azurmendi emphasizes the influence of this deficiency in the very definition of bertsolar-itza: "because we do not know how to define bertsolaritza from the perspective of its output . . . we define it from the perspective of a subject" (Azurmendi 1980, 160). In a later work, Carmen Larra-ñaga echoes Azurmendi's idea and adds an important nuance: those subjects are male bodies, read socially as men (Larrañaga 1994).

And different eras in bertsolaritza have been grounded in the male-bertsolari subject. Joxerra Garzia's classification is the most widely used (Garzia 2012, 51). In that scheme, two periods stand out especially: before and after the twentieth century. Prior to the twentieth century Garzia identifies two eras. On the one hand, what he calls "prehistory" (from the beginning to 1800) and, later, what he terms "Challenges and bertso papers" (in the nineteenth century). On the other, there is the twentieth century, and within that there are several eras: from marginalized bertsolaritza through to the first championship (1900–1935), the period of silence (1936–1945), the bertsolaritza of survival (1945–1960), the bertsolaritza of resistance (1960–1979), from singing to the people to singing for an audience (1980–1998), and multipolar bertsolaritza (1999–present).

If I had to emphasize a key moment in this chronology I would choose the turning point between the nineteenth and twentieth cen-turies, because it was at that moment that the meaning of modern bertsolaritza was established. Subsequently, throughout the twentieth century, there was a revolution (Garzia, Sarasua, and Egaña 2001, 21) in bertsolaritza (especially from the 1980s onward). That is when the tradition was completely modernized until the contemporary definition of bertsolaritza was established, which "creates improvised bertsos in public" (ibid.).

And before forming that definition, within that prehistory (Garzia 2012, 51), what was bertsolaritza? And a bertsolari? The existing testimonies say that bertsolaris appeared in public, going from square to square, street to street. However, as noted, there is little data on that activity and it is almost impossible to know whether they improvised or not, where they did so exactly, when, in front of whom. Nevertheless, returning to Garzia's classification scheme in the transition from the nineteenth to the twentieth centuries, two different kinds of activities related to bertsolaritza existed side by side: on the one hand, the activity surrounding the *bertso-paperak*; and on the other, challenges or *bertso-demak*, mostly within the context of the Floral Games (cultural festivals). In time, bertsolaritza put paper down and gave protagonism to the voice.

Bertso-paperak

In Antonio Zavala's opinion it is difficult to know when the *bertso-papera* genre started (Zavala 1980, 119). It seems like already in the eighteenth century Christmas songs were being printed on paper, but he has his doubts whether these can be considered *bertso-paperak* or not. Indeed, Zavala believes one thing was expressing bertsos on paper by "educated men [sic]" and another bertsos by "natural" bertsolaris. Nevertheless, his hypothesis is that educated people started publishing bertsos on paper and later, seeing it was an appropriate method, bertsolaris (whether educated or not) started doing the same thing. As Zavala himself notes, in Juan Ignazio Iztueta's book *Gipuzkoako probintziaren kondaira* (Account of the province of Gipuzkoa, 1847), it states that the practice of *bertso-paperak* was widespread. Because of that, Zavala's hypothesis is that, while this kind of bertso activity started a century earlier, it gained in popularity in the early nineteenth century. What is more, he says that the two wars (the Carlist Wars) that took place during this time did not affect it adversely (ibid., 120). In the same vein, Maitane Ostolaza's work demonstrates that *bertso-paperak* are an important historiographical source in order to study the development of Carlism through the nineteenth century (Ostolaza 2010, 105). In Ostolaza's opinion, at that time *bertso-paperak* were incredibly popular because they covered many different variables. On the one hand, there was the figure of the bertsolari of that time, a smart, savvy person with a great sensibility toward the preoccupations of the time and, above all, a person of the people with a tremendous capacity for language and words. Because of all this (ibid., 108), "the bertsolaris connected easily with the preoccupations of the people because they within the same ideological and cultural coordinates as the popular classes. From there their acceptance and elevated social status, above all in rural environments, competing in many cases for prestige and influence with the parish priest of the town." On the other hand, *bertso-paperak* fulfilled the need for information that was emerging at that time. The beginning of the modern press as well as the expansion of the publishing business (Aizpuru, Delgado, and Ostolaza 2010, 331) offered *bertso-paperak* new opportunities and duties. Through the expansion of bertsolaritza, they helped the publishing business and *bertso-paperak* give content to the emerging publishing houses.

However, besides spreading information, *bertso-paperak* were also useful in creating and strengthening solidarity and memory (Ostolaza 2010, 109–110). And not just that. Taking into account that these texts were bought, sung, studied, and repeated over and over again, one should also emphasize the participation of the recipients (Aizpuru, Delgado, and Ostolaza 2010, 331), because they could adapt, change, or alter the bertsos. In that way, in the end, bertsos were "no one's and everyone's," transforming into collective creative work: "their definitive authorship belong[ed] to the whole community in that the community gave the final shape to the *bertso-paperak* through successive modifications and adaptations" (ibid.).

Whatever the case, with time, and above all from the 1960s onward, the protagonism of *bertso-paperak* began to wane. At the same time, improvised activity on the part of bertsolaris began to dominate.

Bertsolaritza in Public

Nowadays, according to the traces of information we have, bertsolaritza in public, as a documented and historical subject form, emerged in the nineteenth century. And what is more, not just in any context. But for the first time in the bertso war in Villabona in 1802. And later in the competitions sponsored by the Floral Games.

Following the success of *bertso-paperak*, at one time radio, later television, and now the internet and all the other digital platforms locate bertso activity in the "here and now;" in one specific time and place, in which a voice linked to a body defines an "acoustic space" (Murray 1976). The logic of *bertso-paperak* was different. Bertsos were once written, sold, and distributed with the goal of reading, studying, and repeating them. There was a body, of course, behind that writing, but that disappeared or was erased easily, with the body repeating the bertso gaining the protagonism. There are (specific) bodies behind bertsolaritza in public and on paper. Thus, some specific bodies would be "born" for bertsolaritza in public or on paper.[2]

Placing improvisation front and center has given bertsolaritza a special nature. One can mention many examples but, out of all of them, two should be highlighted. On the one hand, the bertso is a one-off live creation; on the other, the complete connection and feedback that links it with the listeners. On the latter, Joxerra Garzia, Jon Sarasua, and Andoni Egaña (2001, 54) contend that, "In public bertso sessions the participation of the listener is key to the outcome of the gathering: the response of the listener has a clear, key influence on the development of the creation. In the final analysis, the environment is a fundamental ingredient for creation in bertso sessions."

---

2   In order to understand this division in more detail, the work of Pio Perez (2013) on bertsolaris in the Zapirain family is very interesting. There, it is explained clearly that the profile of the Zapirains was very suited to the bertso-papera genre and not so much to performing bertsolaritza in public. Among the difficulties they had in performing public, he especially emphasizes the voice ("it is said they had weak voices").

In practice, the body of the bertsolari is placed front and center: instead of paper, the body supports the bertsolari. At the same time, the body is a boundary between the artist and the recipient. The bertsolari has nothing else to either perceive or to influence. It is difficult for a bertsolari to improvise without an audience; and, at the same time, bertso fans would not be able to receive a bertso without the body of a bertsolari.

In the same way a whole culture was linked to *bertso-paperak*, one can say that improvised bertsolaritza created a new culture, because both bertsolaris and bertso fans had to adapt to new kinds of activities. I am referring to the fact that in this transformation process voice became an indispensable element. The bertsolari, the audience, and the bertso. Those are, today, the fundamental elements in bertsolaritza activity. Those and voice, that which links all of them. Juan Mari Lekuona (1980) remarks that a bertsolari before an audience is the person that "gives voice" to their poems.

Although experts on bertsolaritza theory understand the importance of voice, in general, work on bertsolaritza has located voice within the nature of the song: "the song is also the bertso, and, in creating emotion, the melody could be as important as the text, voice, and the way of singing" (Garzia, Sarasua, and Egaña 2001, 140).

In this paper, I want to rescue the voice from that list of elements (text, melody, voice, and way of singing) in order to highlight its protagonism. Indeed, if we imagine bertsolaritza as the representative of an oral culture, its foundation should be voice. When speaking about oral culture, the anthropologist Joaquín Díaz (2005) says the following about the speaker or the poet:[3] "The sentiment, the myth, the social fabric, are their preferred topics but the delivery of that grinded, shredded, and poetized material only functions if the voice that translates it into intimate language functions with the coincidence of a melody and a rhythm that seduce and fascinate."

The voice necessarily maintains the bertso, and our challenge should be to turn to and study that in an anthropological way.

---

3   Joaquín Díez himself gave me this text. He wrote it for a lecture titled "En defensa de la voz" (In defense of the voice). There is a version of the text online at: https://funjdiaz.net/a_articulos2.php?id=20157.

Anthropology and Voice

It has often happened to me that, in the evening following a bertso session, I go home and cannot get to sleep. I have felt my body full of thrilling emotion, restless, nervous, fidgety, completely taken over. And the voice everywhere. Not able to get it out of my head, a knot made up of different voices. Voices, echoes, the flow of words. I have heard melodies as if whirling around my ears.

With time I get used to it. Moreover, I have learned that those are the remains left over from a bertso session and, like an archeologist, I must do some excavations. The body behaves like a sensograph and collects and registers everything that happens throughout the session. The anthropologist must work around that, collecting and preserving those sensations as best as possible.

As noted, we are *overcome* by different elements and, in practice, we immerse ourselves in a whirl of information and material. Among all of them, and for me included, the 2017 National Bertsolaritza Championship of the Basque Country stood out. Who knows why? During the weeks the championship lasted, voice captured me. As soon as I realized that, I began thinking about the place sounds and voices have had in social anthropology.

Space prevents me here from describing the place listening has had in social anthrophony, but, in general, one can say that from the 1970s and, especially, the 1980s on there have been and continue to be many anthropological studies about sound or listening. In most of those works, the huge attention the West gives to the gaze is highlighted, denouncing the marginalization suffered by listening. Raymond Murray contends that there is belief in 80 percent of the information that appears before our eyes, but that "very few people stop to think that perhaps this was not so true in the past, nor will it be either in the future, and that it is not even so in the case of a large part of the current population of the world" (Murray 1976, 4).

Like Murray, many other authors are in favor of listening, to the point of developing study models like Sound Studies or Sound

Culture Studies. Here, sound ethnographies are developed, defining sound itself in the form of a cultural system (Feld 1990).

However, this chapter seeks to talk about voice rather than sound, setting down both ideas as a starting point. On the one hand, there is the definition of Webb Keane (2001, 268) about voice: "The concept of voice, meaning the linguistic construction of social personae, addresses the question 'Who is speaking?' in any stretch of discourse." From this reflection, I would like to underscore the construction of the nature of voice, in concurrence with the argument of voice expert Amanda Weidman. In her words (Weidman 2014, 40): "voices are material embodiments of social ideology and experience." Out of those approaches, as anthropologists we could choose a clear option: at the point when it is social construction, we must place voice too in its cultural and historical context. And not just that, voice informs us about a context: voice would have a social life (Feld, Fox, Porcello, and Samuels 2004, 341).

These ideas are very clear in the context of oral culture. There, voice takes on another dimension. As Díaz (2005) describes it: voice does not just transmit/develop words, but sentimental content as well. The division that is at the basis of this idea seems necessary to me, because as Leslie C. Dunn and Nancy A. Jones (1994, 1) argue, "voice" and "speech" or discourse are often confused with in most cases speech or discourse taking on the protagonism.

In my opinion, one could also come across traces of that confusion in bertsolaritza. Thus, I would contend that, as time has gone on, it has lost its "oral" nature or/and messages, discourses, and contents have predominated. The reasons are front and center. Contemporary bertsolaris are dependent on communication, its communicative nature. The *glosadores* and *juglars* or troubadours of another age had that same dependence but, as Díaz (2005) explains, everything was subject to voice when he comments on "the effectiveness of their [*juglar*] voices, especially prepared to communicate."

One should not in any way lessen the importance of language, the message, or discourse, but the voice that has transported bertsolaritza to this day out of multiple forms of oral culture and, inevitably, language, the message, and discourse would also be a privileged topic. In order to examine that, anthropology offers different options, always from one specific starting point: namely, that the voice itself has meaning. That meaning is fixed; it is linked to a specific context. Therefore anthropologists must look beyond the universal nature of voice in order to examine where and when they appear, and linked to what and to whom. In this endeavor, the voice assumes its own particular nature. From that point on there are multiple research approaches but for the purposes of this text I would like to highlight two at least: one research field surrounding the ideology of voice and another linked to voice practices.

Voice Ideologies

Voice ideology invites us to consider, in general, the perspectives, meanings, representations, and metaphors developed around voice. In the words of Weidman (2014, 45):

> Ideologies of voice can be characterized as culturally constructed ideas about the voice, including theories of the relationship between vocal quality and character, gender, or other social categories; where the voice comes from; its status in relation to writing and recorded sound; the relationship between the voice and the body; what constitutes a *natural* voice; and who should be allowed to speak and how.

In this vein, Weidman herself highlights the (precise) voice ideology that the West spread with the development of modernity. This, at root, would imply two main ideas. On the one hand, it is emphasized that voice represents someone's presence, an "I," identity as well as agency. In practice, possessing agency would be a synonym for having a voice. On the other, that second idea promoted by the West would be the division between the two basic elements transported by a voice. In Weidman's opinion, from one message to another in a voice, it is customary to separate sound and materiality. In her words (ibid., 39), "*Voice* then becomes a central vehicle for this modern interiorized self."

In any event, the bases of this modern language ideology have also been criticized for a tendency to depart from a universal notion of voice, especially by turning to language and the form of speech. The sonic and material dimension of voice (what Weidman terms "vocality") is typically linked to an animal nature, relegating it to a secondary level or lower. Likewise, with time, psychoanalysis and deconstructivism recovered the full dimensions of voice (as well as its disruptive potential). Thus, Julia Kristeva and especially Roland Barthes explored new perspectives by making interesting new contributions. Among those, I would like to highlight one of Barthes' approaches (Barthes 1977), a basic idea of this paper because it comes from that focus. In his opinion, the pleasure music elicits in the listener does not come so much from the melody or the words or the messages, but instead from the "material vocality" of voice, "the grain of the voice." This grain of the voice brings with it corporal materiality. In doing so, the body itself speaks or sings, Barthes says. Voice would be a fluid emanating from the body and, therefore, it is often possible to see several voices in a body or bodies.[4]

Voice Practices

Connected to voice ideologies, but as a second research field, anthropology emphasizes practices linked to voice because they are what maintain the discourses (representations, metaphors, and so on) about voice. Voice is "created" or "constructed" by means of specific voice practices, with a very close connection emerging between both dimensions. Those practices make reference to the process of voice construction, which Weidman (2014, 42) conceives through the "voicing" concept. In her view, that process would be full of meaning, it would have a strategic and a political nature, and it takes place in performances given in the here and now and in particular places: "Vocal practices, including everyday speech, song, verbal play, ritual speech, oratory, and recitation, can be viewed as

---

4   I have taken this idea from an entry that can be found in a blog titled Flamenco desde el divan (Flamenco from the couch) by Antonio J. Pradel (2014). That entry was titled "El grano y la voz" (The grain and the voice) in which an attempt is made to apply Barthes' ideas to flamenco.

modes of practice and discipline that, in their repeated enactment, may performatively bring into being classed, gendered, political, ethnic, or religious subjects" (Weidman 2014, 44).

Vocal practices include and reflect the tension between the individual and the structure and the influence of each on the other, in several cases also offering alternatives in order to overcome and question that dichotomy. To what extent does voice reveal/reproduce social structure? To what extent is voice capable of influencing social structure? To what extent does voice not help to represent a specific world, with a specific logic, one that escapes that tension between society and individual?

In addition to this practical dimension, such practices have another interesting side: that which puts us into contact with an audience. Indeed, vocal practices have the ability to create listeners. One example of this, among others, is bertsolaritza. As Weidman (ibid.) reminds us, different vocal practices—aided by the diffusion that occurs as a result of repute and often through the media—are able to provide a collectivity with a basic identity, affection, or intimacy.

An example of that would be the affective and intimate connection Basques have had with bertsolaritza through the centuries. The late expert in oral culture Jon Foley said that the development and, above all, social diffusion achieved by bertsolaritza made it a unique global cultural practice.

From an anthropological and ethnographic perspective, we should respect the notion of place. Therein lays our chief task: observing in a specific location. Traditionally, we have represented that location as a (physical) space; hence—following Bronislaw Malinowski—the need to pursue objective research. And hence the need of the anthropologist to approach and integrate. Yet here I am talking about the need that forces those of us seeking to enter (or are interested in entering) the world of sound and voice to go to another kind of location; specifically, that which leads us to the need for another kind of approach and integration. Sound and voice create another space: making/producing sound is making (another kind of) location/place.

The expert in the anthropology of sound Steven Feld describes the work he has undertaken for many years on sounds and voices in the forest in the following way (2004, 465): "And when you hear the way birds overlap in the forest and you hear the way voices overlap in the forest, all of a sudden you can grasp something at a sensuous level that is considerably more abstract and difficult to convey in a written ethnography."

Taking Feld's description as a starting point, I would like to highlight that level that he defines in both a sensual and sensorial way. I would locate that level close to what Nina Sun Eidsheim terms "sensing voice" and it would lead us to inaccessible aspects that (sung) music and voice include: to "those aspects of music that are inaccessible to standard notation but available to all our perceiving senses" (Sun Eidsheim 2015, 134). In Sun Eidsheim's opinion, voice is a window to understanding the physical and sensorial features of both singers' and audiences' bodies. Moreover, it is a window to understanding both singing and listening practices as a lived experience. Likewise, in the "quantitative" methods developed to produce, "write," and express both music and voice, the West has not given any room to those sensorial experiences: "Western music studies favor the idealized and abstract at the expense of the sensible, unrepeatable experience" (ibid.).

That Western system has adjusted (or "tuned") our body and its capacity to perceive sound (Sun Eidsheim 2015, 149). Therefore we have found no way to define or explain what the body (our body) experiences, feels, and experiments when faced with a specific sound or voice.

Women Bertsolaris and Female Voices

As has been stated throughout the text, denaturalized perspectives have been appearing in debates about voice in recent years, especially from language anthropology, musicology, and ethnomusicology. From this perspective, voice appears as a social product that can be constructed, changed, and reconstructed by means of different elements and strategies. Weidman (2014, 39) highlights the contributions of these "perspectives which are grounded in the notion of voice as embodied practice shaped by and embedded in culturally and historically specific social relations."

Starting from that approach, several concepts are emerging that underscore the varied nature of voice: social, subjective, adaptable, and so on. As noted earlier, voice is very closely connected to a specific epistemology in the West. As a result, understanding these opens up numerous possibilities for study and reflection, extending the enormous amount of options voice offers.

Weidman, for example, underscores the importance of the concept of voicing, thereby questioning several ideas that have been considered normal to now. Speakers, Weidman contends, are not closed, completely coherent entities. Mikhail Bakhtin, through his heteroglossia, already noted that different—and frequently contradictory—voices can coexist in one speaker and often in one statement (Bakhtin, quoted in Weidman 2014, 42). At the same time, Weidman argues that the notion of voicing calls into question the idea that the words conveyed by voice mean one subjective experience alone. In her opinion, following Ervin Goffman, the voicing concept underscores the fact that a speaker can have different positions according to the particular kind of "articulation": they can be the "author, or originator of the words; animator, or actual speaker of the words; and principal, the person or entity responsible for the message or in whose interests the words are spoken" (Goffman, quoted in Weidman 2014, 42).

Without doubt, concepts like voicing help to place inner beliefs and ideas about voice in a "natural" way. Moreover, in highlighting the process of voice construction, agency is returned to voice. Above all, to the body transmitted by voice or to the embodied voice. Several authors use the notion of vocality to term this process. Already in the early twentieth century, when authors like Marcel Jousse spoke about orality and oral genres, they gave special importance to the body, because in their opinion it was one of the main keys to producing that link between speaker and audience. In examining Jousse's work, Díaz (2005) emphasizes the importance he gave to the body, in order to make the speaker appear "credible," because he/she was obliged to "chew on and swallow words."

Some years later, the historian Paul Zumthor (1989), faced with the orality versus vocality dichotomy, chose the latter. In his words, "vocality is the historicity of a voice: its use" (Zumthor 1989, 23).

Those that have studied orality in depth are clear that if the word is strong and influential, it is because the speaker *lives* that word. Besides the message words extend, there must be a connection between the word and life, and that implicates the person—in their entirety—appearing before an audience: "Because, as Zumthor would say, the conduct of the performer implicates their whole person: knowledge, intelligence, sensibility, nerves, muscles, respiration, a talent for reworking in a very short space of time" (Zumthor, quoted in Díaz 2005).

Going one step further, Leslie C. Dunn and Nancy A. Jones (1994) represent voice as a form of cultural construction that coincides with gender, and not just in a metaphorical way: but, rather, in the form of an embodied or corporally constructed (gendered) process.

> To move from "voice" to "vocality," then, implies a shift from a concern with the phenomenological roots of voice to a conception of vocality as a cultural construct. By specifying female vocality, we also assert the centrality of gender in shaping that construction. Here our third term, "embodiment" comes into play. As a material link between "inside" and "outside," self and other, the voice is, in Nelly Furman's works, the locus of articulation of an individual's body to language and society (Dunn and Jones 1994, 2).

I think that women bertsolaris have spent the last five centuries trying to find their voice/sound again; that of the *profazadorak* from the fifteenth century; that which Maialen Lujanbio embodied at the 2017 Bertsolari Championship of the Basque Country when she took the audience back to the radical orality of the fifteenth century.

Nowadays, it is very difficult for us to write about or imagine a society or culture that had few options when it came to writing (Frenk

1997, 15). Yet women profazadorak, those who were banned by a fifteenth-century decree by the Provincial Council of Bizkaia, were close to such a situation. We know that writing was quite prevalent in the West at that time, but as Margit Frenk (ibid., 30) says, the voice, orality, and vocality still "prevailed" (at least until the end of the fifteenth century). And not just any voice, orality, or vocality, but that which was made up of corporal materiality. In order to portray how this was, I would like to return to the abovementioned decree. That ban defined its target in the following way (Garzia, Sarasua, and Egaña 2001, 19): "women, known for being shameful, and agitators of peoples, they make couplets and songs in an infamous and libelous manner." Previously, those women's activity had been described thus (ibid.):

> How one can lament and mourn the dead . . . They ordered, and established by law, that hereafter, when one wishes to mourn for a deceased person in Bizkaia . . . no person shall dare make lamentations pulling on their hair, or scratching their face, or unveiling their head, nor shall they make singing lamentations, nor mourn in jargon, under pain of payment of one thousand coins for each person acting in contrary and every time.

In order to understand these descriptions, Frenk's explanation of what communication consisted of in that universe of orality is useful (Ong 1982; Finnegan 1992; Zumthor 1997, quoted in Frenk 1997, 34): "in an oralized culture *communication* brings together people in groups . . . and *performance*—a word that is essential in this context—is necessary for the full carrying out of a text . . . so the *hic et nunc* of that public and collective event takes on full importance."

This, says Frenk (ibid., 35), means that in a situation in which poetry is read out or sung, the singer, the audience, the place, and the moment are indispensable elements of that event. And bodies are at the center of that event. A body guiding another or many others. In that context, the *word* is alive, it has a very real nature, it has a present. The materiality of that voice is, specifically, its power, message, discourse, that which words overcome.

Therefore one could speculate that, as regards the profazadorak, beyond their words or songs, the ban established was aimed at their bodies. That is why the people behind the decree spent so much time describing their corporal activity. The sensorial and sensual flowed from those bodies in their laughs, intense gestures, and tendency to go unveiled.

It was a case of prohibiting and castigating a voice/sound. A materiality. Produced by some (specific) bodies.

We do not know who produced that decree, nor anything about the trajectory of those profazadorak, but we do know that from that point on we almost lose trace of women bertsolaris. We can be sure that, following the ban, women (like men) still made use of bertsos to continue relating to the world around them, but very few bertsos tell us anything about that. They refer to single episodes or news items; often with nameless protagonists.

The following documented bertso activity dates from 1802, in the town square of Villabona, Gipuzkoa. Jesus Mari Etxezarreta offers the following account of what happened (Etxezarreta 1993, 10):

> In 1801 in the main square of Villabona. The bertsolaris taking part: Juan Ignacio de Zabala, from Amezketa and José Joaquin de Erroicena "Txabalategi" from Hernani. The bet, five ounces of gold each (ten ounces of gold in total). The season: around carnival time (February). It was said around four thousand listeners gathered. There were also judges: each side chose one person, then another "impartial" person (the mayor, a man of the cloth...). The spent two hours in the activity.

This description has nothing to do with the implications of the decree. In this case, the person describing the event pays attention to the formal conditions of the "performance," always underscoring its competitive nature: a long two-hour contest for money between two (male) bertsolaris, before judges and a large audience. The bodies disappear and, with them, the voices.

No woman is mentioned at this early nineteenth-century session, but at the close of that same century, we know that women bertsolaris were active as part of the Floral Games. As noted earlier, competition was at the heart of this festival (Toledo 1998). As the chronicles say, women bertsolaris at that time "hardly dared take part" (Izaga 2017).

That said, there were some who won competitions, such as Marieder Uthurralt in 1894. Although the press of the time said she was an excellent improviser, it was surprised because "the weaker sex prevailed over the stronger sex." Among those words, it makes little sense referring to strength but that allows us to measure the thinking of the time: women were already the weaker sex and males powerful in all areas.

Bertsolaris and the main features of their activity would be fulfilled through these competitions. In the end, the first National Bertsolari Championship was held in 1935. At that time, twenty bertsolaris from all over the Basque Country came together, without any elimination rounds. They were all men. The second championship was held in 1936. Later, as a result of the Franco regime, there was a break of over twenty years. Ultimately, Euskaltzaindia (the Academy of the Basque Language) took over the organization of the National Championship of the Basque Country in 1960, which was followed by championships in 1962, 1965, and 1967. Then there was a break again until 1980. At that time bertsolaritza was in the middle of a renovation process. The Association of Friends of Bertsolaritza would be created and it was responsible for organizing the 1980 championship (and the following ones). Xabier Amuriza was the championship winner at the time, making several noteworthy contributions. Among these, his most well-known was to design and found bertso schools. Amuriza claimed with some certainty that people were not born bertsolaris, but they could be trained to be so. People could be trained to take part in bertsolaritza, to become bertsolaris.

That idea has had a pronounced importance in the process of women stepping up to the stage. To that time there was no "mixed" bertsolaritza; it was almost impossible for women and men to appear alongside each other in the bertso world, in front of an audience at least. The bertso schools made that possible, on the one hand because women started to learn there and, on the other, because those spaces legitimized women and men appearing alongside each other in bertsolaritza.

It was through the bertso schools that women's names started appearing in bertsolaritza: Kristina Mardaras, Arantzazu Loidi, Maialen Lujanbio, Iratxe Ibarra, Estitxu Arozena, Oihane Perea, Ainhoa Agirreazaldegi, Oihane Enbeita, Estitxu Eizagirre, and so on. Mardaras is the oldest of these women and she describes that time, when women started appearing in public for the first time, in the following way:

> At that time women were mothers, or virgins, or spinsters, or one of those in the San Francisco neighborhood of Bilbao [prostitutes]. No sir, sorry, but what world do you live in? You have thousands of different kinds of women around you, to speak about normally. And in bertso themes, of course, it was funny, well, not for me. And they were slow to pick up on that.[5]

Until then, there was just one model of bertsolari and bertsolaritza, developed by men and represented by men. That was reflected in bodies that appeared on stage. One specific body, and with that one way of appearing with one voice and arms, hands, a back, a chest, and legs, for many years the only one. In practice one could say that preoccupations with the body appeared when women started to take the stage.

Carmen Larrañaga's diagnosis at the time could not be any clearer (Aristi 1995): there was no place for femininity in bertsolaritza; for women yes, but in exchange for masculinity. One women bertsolari came to a similar conclusion in an interview: Question: In your opinion is the body an element in play in bertsolaritza? "Yes, even if you don't want that. For me, always, my strategy has been conceal, I mean, as if this [pointing to her body] wasn't there, what a handicap it is."[6]

---

5   Personal interview with Kristina Mardaras, Villabona (Gipuzkoa), November 25, 2010.
6   Personal interview with a woman bertsolari, Villabona (Gipuzkoa), June 16, 2010.

To be a women taking part in bertsolaritza was an obstacle, and especially wanting to appear like a woman (physically, esthetically, in the way of dressing, and so forth). Sometimes, when there was a chance of making a joke, women who had become skilled at creating bertsos offered their bertso partners an easy escape. Because of that, in the traditional context of bertsolaritza it seemed a risk to emphasize oneself (physically) as a woman. As a result, girls who went into bertsolaritza imitated their male bertso partners, especially at the outset.

For some, on the contrary, that strategy was very difficult to follow.

Arantzazu Loidi was very young[7] when she began in the world of bertsolaritza and, from that point on, she appeared in numerous public sessions with the best bertsolaris of the day. She took part in several championships and won some of them, but there was something in her presence that reminded listeners over and over again of her condition as a *woman*: voice. In some people's opinion, it was too high-pitched. One bertso aficionado told me the following regarding Loidi's singing: "Arantzazu didn't have a good voice, didn't have a good throat, she was a lot more feminine in that regard compared to Maialen Lujanbio."

Arantzazu Loidi herself recalls several moments that clearly reflect the reactions her presence elicited:[8]

> I remember once at that time when I was still at school . . . how someone, a man, came up to me and said: "I'll never get used to listening to a woman." It was for me like huh? I mean, it made me conscious of the fact I was a woman and... but I didn't experience it like that. I didn't define myself like that, yet I realized just how much of an obstacle that was.

---

7   As Arantzazu Loidi told me, she was taking part in public recitals and sessions at the age of fourteen. Interview with Arantzazu Loidi, Villabona (Gipuzkoa), October 29, 2010.

8   Ibid.

And in most cases in which she performed as a bertsolari her voice became a topic of conversation:

> And at the beginning . . . I had to break down a wall or something like that, I don't know how to say it... a boundary... that opposition to listening to a woman's voice. A little girl in the bertso world, that is, a bertsolari, and what's more a little girl or a child and what's more a girl. And besides, with that kind of voice because I had a certain voice, just that... I heard that a lot.

Yet as noted earlier, at that time when Loidi's voice was being heard (the 1980s) bertsolaritza was in the middle of an unstoppable renovation process and as part of that, as well as the novelty of women's participation in general, they were also innovators: in general, women bertsolaris were a part of the transformation process that was taking place (Gartzia, Sarasua, and Egaña 2001, 28).

At that time, several profiles were evidently taking shape: women, young people, university students, urban Basques, and so on. But in the case of women, that process would have a specific consequence: the lack of an identity or profile.

In time, trying to be a woman in bertso sessions gradually started to seem more normal; it was something "original" and organizers tried to include a woman bertsolari in their line-ups. As women themselves note, with the exception of a few names, the rest of these women appeared as in some way "mutually interchangeable" They only existed as a collective: "We, the women bertsolaris," nameless, without any nuance, any one of them able to replace the other.

Celia Amorós (1987) captures this situation perfectly when she speaks about "the space of identicals." In this case she takes Søren Kierkegaard's words as a starting point (Amorós 1987, 120): "The woman is an infinite creature and, as a consequence, a collective being: the woman encompasses in herself all women."

This "space of identicals" was juxtaposed with the "space of equals." Men achieve expectation among themselves in that "space of equals" (Amorós 1987,121):

By space of equals we understand in this context the gravitational field of political forces defined by those who exercise power, acknowledging themselves as legitimate holders of the social contract, while at the same time they recognize the expectation of other potential title-holders who wait their turn in the role of trainees, who are not currently exercising such power but are on the waiting list for an always achievable changeover, at least in principle.

From the moment of expectation on there is acknowledgement, the subject can be honored, power, prestige. Each man in the "space of equals" (Amorós only portrays men in this space) has his own profile, his own features, his own nature, his own distinctive features. He is known because of them. And among them—even if in competition—they conceive of one another as colleagues. That is how the genealogies of male bertsolaris have been formed as well. Individuals in their own right make up the contemporary course of bertsolaritza and anecdotes, stories, compliments, and so on are often heard about each of them. That has been termed the history of bertsolaritza.

A crack appeared in that lineal history on December 13, 2009. On that day, Maialen Lujanbio won the National Bertsolaritza Championship of the Basque Country. That day has been interpreted as historic from the perspective of the history of bertsolaritza and, in several people's opinion, from the perspective of Basque culture in general. While many different interpretations have been made and can be made about that championship, one stands out above all others: its referential power. It was an acknowledgement, it was an expectation, honor, prestige. Following that championship more women came into bertsolaritza, to make their voices heard and to begin and carry on being skilled in creating bertsos. And the Association of Friends of Bertsolaritza coincided with that new emerging subject, designing and creating several new initiatives.[9] Little by

---

9   For example, a gender group was created within the association in 2008. Some years later, in 2015, the empowerment bertso school was set up. Prior to these two "formal" initiatives, one can interpret as a watershed moment the first meeting of women bertsolaris in 2003. Besides all that, in recent years several initiatives have been undertaken in order to promote women's involvement in bertsolaritza.

little, feminism took to the stage, creating an echo in debates about gender equality in society.

Meanwhile, the National Bertsolaritza Championship of the Basque Country was held again in 2013, and won by a man, Amets Arzallus. Many experienced this as a defeat for those advocating change in the championship dynamic. And they would, specifically, be forced to wait until the next championship in 2017.

And on October 30, 2017, 2,260 of us gathered at the Irun sports center heard the theme-prompter (the person who presents the bertsolari with a scenario around which verses will be created) say, "everything was fine, until the light was switched on." It was part of the "prison work" exercise (in which bertsolaris must improvise on the same topic and so as they do not hear the others' bertsos, they must remain out of earshot in a "prison cell"); and it was Maialen Lujanbio's turn, following on from two other bertsolaris who had already improvised on the same theme.

Lujanbio improvised three excellent bertsos in order to respond to the topic,[10] brilliantly combining content, technique, and form of singing. Outstanding. However, that brilliance cannot just be explained in terms of the success achieved socially by that group of bertsos. In the days that followed, a video of the performance circulated on social media, and the session was much written and talked about. Moreover, those of us who witnessed the session first-hand spent the days that followed reflecting on how we felt and experienced it. Literally reflecting. Indeed, returning to Jousse's idea, the words used by Lujanbio in that bertso session offered the audience something to "chew on and swallow."[11]

---

10   In order to respond to the topic suggested, Lujanbio portrayed a story of an emotional-sexual encounter between a transsexual and a (male) heterosexual. The man, who was under the impression he was starting out on relations with a woman, realizes it was someone (a transsexual) with a male body when the light is switched on. The basis of Lujanbio's bertsos is made up of the transsexual's response at this surprise. And in this case, Lujanbio was singing from the transsexual's point of view.

11   This set of bertsos is available online (last seen October 26, 2018) at https://www.youtube.com/watch?v=xYeCYRTrSFg https://bertsoa.eus/bertsoak/14800-kartzela-maialen-lujanbio-btn17. I would recommend taking a look to get some visual idea of my description of the event.

Personally, I was drenched to my skin with that feeling and emotion, for some time.

How can one comprehend the connection between that set of bertsos and the audience? How can one explain the effect of that group of rhymed words? In my opinion, if what happened is not explained in both a sensual and sensorial way, it is difficult.

Maialen Lujanbio, her bertsos, her form of bertsos, and especially her voice transported us back to the fifteenth century. To that long dark era in which voice was the main and almost only means for a person to express, present, and discern something. In that long dark era in which it was one (and almost the only) space for sound and voice to come together, to live. The time when bodies were under the control of and at the service of voices. Bodies used voice to attract other bodies, and bodies came together and coexisted in voice. Voice was a means of both suffering and enjoying.

Lujanbio demonstrated the ability and skill of the *juglars* of old: "people who transmitted a commitment—that of communicating wisdom—through their voice, which enveloped listeners and elevated them above reality, while at the same time highlighting their belonging to a land and a culture" (Díaz 2005).

Like the first women bertsolaris, like those punished and proscribed profazadorak, Lujanbio's voice transported us back to those (gendered) bodies bertsolaritza had, in which words, reasons, and discourses remained on a secondary level, and voice created through body merged with the voice of listeners, becoming one single speaker.

Sun Eidsheim offers an excellent description of an underwater concert given by the singer and performance artist Julia Snapper. She demonstrates clearly the corporal dimension of listening; the sound produced by the singer underwater (and especially the "waves" this creates) is felt directly within the bodies of the audience, both becoming one physically: "In effect, at an underwater performance where the audience and performers are immersed, the singer's body, the water, and the audiences' bodies become one vibrating mass, a single pulsating speaker" (Sun Eidsheim 2015, 148).

I believe the experience described by Sun Eidsheim is valid to describe the scenario experienced in Irun.[12]

There we were, bertsolari and audience, by the ocean, submerged in the waves, water up to our knees, gasping for breath, waiting for the high tide of voice to inundate us all.

Following a long period of punishment, the body had returned to bertsolaritza.

Bibliography

Aizpuru, Mikel Xabier, Ander Delgado, and Maitane Ostolaza. 2010. "Pueblo, política y nación en el País Vasco (1833–1936): una aproximación a través de los bertso-paperak."In *Procesos de nacionalización en la España contemporánea*, edited by Mariano Esteban de Vega and Mª Dolores De la Calle. Salamanca: Universidad de Salamanca.

Amorós, Celia. 1987. "Espacio de los iguales, espacio de las idénticas: notas sobre poder y principio de individuación." *Arbor: Ciencia, pensamiento y cultura* 503–504: 113–28.

Aristi, Pako. 1995. "Bertsolaritza feminismoaren begietatik begiratuta." *Bertsolari Aldizkaria* 17: 2–9.

Azurmendi, Joxe. 1980. "Bertsolaritzaren estudiorako." *Jakin* 14–15: 139–64.

12　Coincidentally, Jorge Oteiza also used water to portray the bertsolari's activity, and the relationship between bertsolari and audience. Here is how he describes it (2007, 117): ""The bertsolari's technique is that s/he is in front of everyone and disappears into her/his inner reality. From where her/his words emerge (and will continue to emerge). I usually say that it is as if s/he allows himself to be submerged in a river (the river of his internal vision). Now I also say that it is as if s/he abandons the audience (that is listening to him) on a beach. And s/he walks backward toward the ocean. And, completely submerged, s/he speaks to us in that watery rhyme that comes to us on waves hitting the shore (which can also be rough)." As Asier Altuna once said in an interview, this description is at the root of the documentary *Bertsolari* and, naturally, one can see it "performed" in the film itself.

———. 1990. "Bertsolaritzaren kontzeptuari buruz." In Xabier Amuriza et al. *Bertsolaritza, formarik gabeko heziketa.* Bilbao: UPV-EHU.

Barthes, Roland. 1977. "The Grain of the Voice." In *Image, Music, Text.* Essays selected and translated by Stephen Heath. New York: Noonday Press.

Díez, Joaquín. 2005. "En defensa de la voz." Online article at Fundación Joaquín Díaz. At https://funjdiaz.net/a_articulos2.php?id=20157 (last accessed September 24, 2018).

Dunn, Leslie C., and Nancy A. Jones, eds. 1994. *Embodied Voices: Representing Female Vocality in Western Culture.* Cambridge: Cambridge University Press.

Etxezarreta, Jesus Mª. 1993. *Bertsolarien desafioak, guduak eta txapelketak.* Donostia: Sendoa Argitaletxea.

Feld, Steven, Aaron A. Fox, Thomas Porcello, and David Samuels. 2004. "Vocal Anthropology: From the Music of Language to the Language of Song." In *A Companion to Linguistic Anthropology,* edited by Alessandro Duranti. Oxford: Blackwell.

Feld, Steven, and Donald Brenneis. 2004. "Doing Anthropology in Sound." *American Ethnologist* 31, no. 4: 461–74.

Finnengan, Ruth. 1992. *Oral Poetry: Its Nature, Significance, and Social Context.* Bloomington and Indianapolis: Indiana University Press.

Frenk, Margit. 1997. *Entre la voz y el silencio: la lectura en tiempos de Cervantes.* Alcalá de Henares: Ediciones del Centro de Estudios Cervantinos.

Garzia, Joxerra. 2012. *Bertsolaritza.* Donostia: Etxepare Euskal Institutua.

Garzia, Joxerra, Jon Sarasua, and Andoni Egaña. 2001. *Bat-Bateko bertsolaritza. Gakoak eta azterbideak.* Donostia: Bertsozale Elkartea.

Hernández García, Jone M. 2016. "Odolak badu generorik? Edo zergatik gorputz emeak ez diren bertsoetarako bizitoki." In *Etnografia feministak Euskal Herrian. XXI. mendera begira dagoen antropología*, edited by Mari Luz Esteban and Jone M. Hernández García. Bilbao: UPV/EHU; UEU.

—————. 2017. "¿Acaso tiene género la sangre? O por qué los cuerpos femeninos no sirven como habitáculo para los versos." In *Etnografías feministas. Una mirada al siglo XXI desde la antropología vasca*, edited by Mari Luz Esteban and Jone M. Hernández García. Barcelona: Ediciones Bellaterra.

Izaga, Xabier. 2017. "Emakumeen oinen bila." *GAUR8* May 20: 12–13. At https://www.naiz.eus/eu/hemeroteca/gaur8/editions/gaur8_2017-05-20-07-00.pdf (last accessed October 26, 2018).

Keane, Webb. 2001. "Voice." In *Key Terms in Language and Culture*, edited by Alessandro Duranti. Oxford: Blackwell.

Murray, Raymond. 1976. "El mundo del sonido. Los sonidos del mundo." *El Correo. UNESCO (año XXIX)* (November): 4–8.

Larrañaga, Carmen. 1994. "Bertsolarismo: habitat de la masculinidad." *Bitarte* 4: 29–51.

Lekuona, Juan Mari. 1980. "Jendaurreko betsolaritza." *Jakin* 14–15: 99–113.

Ong, Walter J. 1982. *Oralidad y Escritura: Tecnologías de la palabra*. Translated by Angélica Scherp. México, D. F.: Fondo de Cultura Económica.

Ostolaza, Maitane. 2010. "La cultura carlista a través de la literatura popular: los 'bertso paperak'." In *Las culturas políticas en la España del siglo XIX*, edited by Julien Lanes Marsall and Maitane Ostolaza. Paris: Editions Hispaniques.

Oteiza, Jorge. 2007. *Quousque Tandem*. Alzuza: Fundación Museo Oteiza.

Perez, Pio. 2013. *Joxe Zapirainen bertso-malkoak*. Amorebieta: Labayru Ikastegia.

Pradel, Antonio J. 2014. "El 'grano de la voz' del cante." *Flamenco desde el diván*. Blog. Plataforma Independiente de Estudios Flamencos Modernos y Contemporáneos, Universidad Internacional

de Andalucía, October 26. At http://www.pieflamenco.com/
el-grano-de-la-voz-del-cante/ (last accessed April 21, 2018).

Sun Eidsheim, Nina. 2011. "Sensing Voice." *The Sense and Society* 6, no.
2: 133–55.

Surralles, Alexandre. 1998. "Entre el pensar y el sentir. La antropología
frente a las emociones." *Anthropologica* 16: 291–304.

———.2009a. *En el corazón del sentido*. Lima: IFEA/IWGIA.

———. 2009b. "De la intensidad o los derechos del cuerpo. La afec-
tividad como objeto y como método." *Runa* 1: 29–44.

Toledo, Ana Mª. 1998. "Antonie d'Abbadie Hegoaldean (1879–1895)."
In *Antoine d'Abbadie, 1897–1997. Congrès International. Eusko
Ikaskuntza*. Conference proceedings. Bilbao: Eusko Ikaskunt-
za.

Villaverde, Teresa. 2016. "Las ideologías de la Voz." *Pikara Online Ma-
gazine*, July 28. At http://www.pikaramagazine.com/2016/07/
las-ideologias-de-la-voz/ (last accessed September 24, 2018).

Weidman, Amanda. 2014. "Anthropology and Voice." *Annual Review of
Anthropology* 43: 37–51.

Zavala, Antonio. 1980. "Bertso paperak." *Jakin* 14–15: 115–33.

Zumthor, Paul. 1983. *Introducción a la poesía oral*. Madrid: Taurus.

———. 1989. *La letra y la voz. De la "literatura" medieval*. Madrid: Cát-
edra.

CHAPTER 2

Women in Bertsogintza: From Being a Subject to Being Capable

Oihana Iguaran Barandiaran

Bertsolaritza interprets its reality and context in terms of sudden improvisation, and in order to seek out delight, reflection and/or provocation on the part of listeners. It can take place on the basis of freely chosen or set themes (in the latter case, as well as a theme, the bertsolari may also be given a personality or situation to improvise on). Until the 1980s, bertsolaris performing in front of audiences in public were men. The presence of women,[1] besides being listeners (and nor were there any there either), was limited to mentions or characters improvised by bertsolaris according to bertsogintza. Women, then, appeared in bertsos as the subject of a song or a character to interpret. However, in recent years women bertsolaris

---

1   Throughout this work, the word "woman" will make reference to those people classified socially as a woman; and "man," meanwhile, to those as a man.

have brought their own voices to the public arena. Change is happening little by little; there is, then, still much to do.

In her work on bertsogintza, Carmen Larrañaga offers some reasons why women were not found in the public bertso sphere until relatively recently. Larrañaga contends that bertsolaritza is constructed and expressed as a masculine practice, and on that basis, "women only seem to fit in as objects conceived by men, or as mere transmitters of compositions by them" (Larrañaga 1995, 409). Lorea Agirre, likewise, sees that feature in the definition of the bertsolari by Joxerra Garzia, Andoni Egaña, and Jon Sarasua (2001): "at least the definition has another important adjective within it: the bertsolari is a man who creates improvised bertsos in from of people." In Agirre's opinion, man is "an adjective, or perhaps a noun as well" (Agirre 2010, 46). Larrañaga (1997, 61) defines the bertsolari in the same vein: "the bertsolari is a man who performs spontaneously and in a public setting. In other words, a *plazagizona* [public figure/man]." Today, women bertsolaris are part of the chief public spaces but at the time Larrañaga was writing, in the late 1990s, that was unfortunately not the case. She continues: "the history of bertsolaritza to the present has barely included or examined the presence of women, and what is more, the bertsolari in that social imaginary, now and two hundred years ago, is male" (Larrañaga 1997, 59). Special efforts are being made in education and in transmission to reinforce that presence but, taking in account the fact that the image we have of the bertsolari is one constructed on the main stages, it still has not changed a lot.

Nowadays, one can see women bertsolaris in public activities and it looks like a contemporary thing; and yet one could ask the question: where were women bertsolaris before? The truth of the matter is that, if one looks at testimonies, we see that women have always been involved. For example, the first references are recorded in Pedro Lemonauria's (1837, 12) legal collection on the 1452 old law of Bizkaia "concerning Women, who are known to be shameless, seditious people in localities, they compose verses, and songs in a libelous inflammatory way" and the text highlights a prohibition on them. The fact that Larrañaga (1995, 421) reveals that women bertsolaris are unknown individually is worth underscoring, moreover, because all references to them are generic or because they are linked to other bertsolaris in their wider families: "she is blurred through a parental reference that stems from the men in their families that emerged with their own names."

Women have also created bertsos in families that have been well known for being bertsolaris, and we know this only thanks to the testimonies of the bertsolaris. Larrañaga (1995, 420), for example, cites Inocencio Olea revealing his sister's talent: "At home yes, but outside home, forget it. If a woman had been singing bertsos at that time, she wouldn't get married." Likewise, the bertsolari Patxi Etxeberria, in an interview for the online journal *bertsoa* (Labaka 2017), confesses that his sister was the most skillful bertsolari in their family home. Moreover, Etxeberria also recalls how his brother once mentioned that the bertsolari "Gaztelu" said that, of the three of them, his sister was the best at home and if she would have had an opportunity to perform in public she would have been a really good bertsolari.

Consequently, it is important to stress that there have always been women bertsolaris, even if they did not make much of an impact. Agirre (2010, 10) sums it up thus: "Women bertsolaris do not come from nowhere, but rather from a tradition of being condemned to secrecy, from a tradition of lacking importance," and this was not a situation particular to bertsolaritza, but something that happened in "all public and private activities throughout history."

Larrañaga (1995, 420) sums up in one sentence the different roles of women and men in bertsolaritza: "They [women] collaborate in maintaining the tradition while the men create it." As she observes in the introduction, "tradition has limited women to the work of transmission, while it has equipped men for being a brighter pro-tagonist and creator" (Larrañaga 1995, 407). And as noted above, Agirre also highlights the aforementioned punishment, thanks to which that differentiation has been maintained. Nevertheless, achieving that "transmitter" status is very interesting because that is, according to tradition (and by order of the gender system), the work that many women have done within the sphere of the home:

transmission. Whether the language itself, stories, songs, old bert-sos, and so forth, historical accounts have remained intact thanks to kitchen transmission. Larrañaga's account, for example, of such a well-known bertsolari as Manuel Lasarte (1927–2012), is striking. Specifically, he believed that he had learned bertsolaritza by himself, that he had begun improvising as a child, without considering the fact that it could have been connected to the bertsos his mother sang to him every day.[2]

In the final analysis, just as Patxi Etxeberria says what the case was among the siblings in his home, in many other homes women and men learned to create bertsos by studying from each other. On the way to public performance, however, the spectacle was in the hands of just one of the genders. The acclaim of many for women's ability to improvise went against, however, the manner in which the voices were separated in public: "the ability to improvise with which women are recognized in the private sphere, and that contrasts so emphatically with the absence of their voices in public, without mentioning the severe segregation of spaces that keeps men and women apart in the practice of bertsolaritza" (Larrañaga 1995, 420). The result of all this has been to view bertsolaritza as a male tradition. Agirre (2010, 13) explains how male bertsolaris fulfil a "hegemonic model" with their sole presence, concluding "and therefore his image is always 'neutral'. The lack of presence of male bertsolaris would be transformational, were it to happen."

If the male presence is neutral, women's would be groundbreak-ing, in the event it did not maintain the same form as that of men. Agirre argues that, following her interviews with women bertsolaris, the male bertsolari model has been valued like that:

> The context, the system, leave them no other way. Only the hegemonic group's form of speech (index, code, aes-thetics, ethics) is in force in the public space, and there-fore women bertsolaris have had to embrace that form

---

2   "The response of Manuel Lasarte (an improviser born in Leitza in 1927) to the question of how he came to bertsolaritza: 'I began to sing verses before I was four years old. By myself. When we were children, in our home, our mother was a big fan . . . Mother sang a lot, a great many things" (Larrañaga 1995, 13).

of speech (like a kind of transvestitism). If they do not use that form of speech, the hegemonic model does not "understand" the women's form of speech (index, code, aesthetics, ethics). That misunderstanding is just a way of ensuring the subordination of women (Agirre 2010, 49).

To the extent that the hegemonic model in the public sphere is male, the result is a public discourse constructed by men and for men (including the linguistic register that goes along with the discourse). In the face of that, women do not have any registers or codes with which to develop topics that may be of special importance to them. Agirre uses muted group theory (Ardener and Ardener 1975) to explain the lack of a register or code, thereby understanding women bertsolaris as a muted group within bertsogintza. In her opinion, one can see this "in a specific kind of humor; in a way of making up the discourse; in the method of doing competitions; in the dominance of some specific terms and symbols" (Agirre 2010, 19). And in order to stop being a muted group it is essential for women bertsolaris to create their own register and code. Following Ardener and Ardener, this change would involve moving from a "model of women" to constructing a "women's model."

Even though women have not been present on stage, bertsolaritza has sung to women and what is more, it has addressed women in depth in many topics. If, following Ardener and Ardener, we distinguish between the model of women and the women's model, it would be a question of paying attention to concepts that women "create" about themselves rather than the multiple ideas that represent women for male bertsolaris. When it comes to bertsolaris' work voicing roles and topics in society, in their work *Gai-jartzailearen eskuliburua* (The theme prompter's handbook) the theme prompters Xabino San Sebastian, Inazio Usarralde, and Nikolas Zeberio state the following: "we have often assigned young male bertsolaris the role of mother, wife, grandmother, or sister, and they have sung without any problem" (San Sebastian; Usarralde eta Zeberio 2002, 15). And immediately after, likewise, they claim that is the same the other way around. But playing out a role and signing outside of one's own experience is not the same thing. That is how Maialen Lujanbio recalls it too, in an interview with Agirre:

> When we started performing in public, many topics took on a very real dimension. In other words, until then men interpreted all women. Now we ... and although bertso-laritza gained in the realist dimension, they defined us. We spent years being mothers, being daughters, being grandmothers, being girlfriends... and normally those female characters were rarely portrayed; now, too, male characters are portrayed in much more detail, and so in the topics the protagonist is a male character and the female character is a little bit more secondary and contrasting (Lujanbio, in Agirre 2010, 17).

As a result, women bertsolaris are capable of portraying women's voices in a more real way, but not, more generally, of representing women; even less when it comes to defining them. First, the scarce stage presence and very differentiation of registers implies a lot of a work and a major contribution. As Agirre (2010, 48) states, "the presence, activity, praxes, and consciousness of women bertsolaris is busy proposing and establishing a new alternative. They are busy creating a new definition from within bertsolaritza itself."

The change, on the other hand, goes beyond what we will measure with the Bechdel test. In this study it will be possible to analyze women's presence; but, after reading the studies of Agirre (2010) and Larrañaga(1995), it is clear that, beyond mere presence of women bertsolaris, "a new lead, a new form of speech, a new index, a way of creating, and a new outcome are being proposed" (Agirre 2010, 4). Nevertheless, one cannot ignore the importance that presence has, because the appearance of another kind of "aesthetics and ethics" in that traditionally solely male model has a symbolic significance, especially as a on the main stages that make up the sample.

The Research Questions

The goal of this study is to analyze the presence of women (both in person and as characters) on the main stages of bertsogintza. As the main public spaces have been defined as championship finals and bertso days, the period has been delimited as that between the National Championship of 1986 and the present day. Consequently, the first research question is: (RQ_1) How present have women's voices been in public during the previous thirty years? The Bechdel test about and linked to men will address that presence and, therefore, we will be able to quantify a minimum identity level of women's voices from one session to the next. There are, however, changes outside the count as well.

The second question is addressed to see what has changed: the quality of those women's voices in public as well as the kinds and levels of definitions of female characters: (RQ_2) Thus, how has the presence of women in public influenced the representation of female voices?

Methodology

In order to measure how women's presence and voices have been represented in the main public bertso spaces, a survey based on the Bechdel test has been applied to the main public bertso spaces since the mid-1980s. In order to do that, the individual championship finals have been taken into account, whether provincial or national; as well as the main bertso day festivals as well. The following paragraphs explain the reasons for choosing this test, specifications, and samples.

The Bechdel Test

It is also known as the Bechdel-Wallace test (although it was first published by Alison Bechdel, she credited the idea first to Liz Wallace). It was created with the aim of describing how gender was portrayed in fiction, originally in order to visualize gender exclusion in movies. It first appeared in the 1985 comic book *Dykes to Watch Out For* in a strip titled "The Rule."[3] In the strip, a woman tells her friend that she only decides to watch a movie if it fulfills

---

3   Alison Bechdel, "The Rule," in *Dykes to Watch Out For* (1985), at http://dykestowatchoutfor.com/the-rule.

a rule, based on three questions: Are there at least two women in the movie? Do they talk to each other? And, do they talk about something else besides a man?

Bechdel was possibly inspired by Virginia Woolf's *A Room of One's Own*, which, in chapter 5, states: "I tried to remember any case in the course of my reading where two women are represented as friends. . . . They are now and then mothers and daughters. But almost without exception they are shown in their relation to men" (Woolf 1929, 53).

The test has its limits, because one cannot resolve whether there is sexist content or not in a fictional work; yet women have projected a "sovereign" presence in it (in other words, without being based on any relationship to men). On the other hand, the way of defining a character or conversation can also change the outcome of the test. Therefore, more than a general rule, one must understand the Bechdel-Wallace test as a foundation, an idea to gauge to what extent there is gender or other kinds of marginalization in fiction. Specifically, the outcomes of this test have also been used in terms of race, functional diversity, and sexuality, in order to analyze characters in depth; or example, at the www.racialbechdel. tumblr.com website, the test is applied to movies and series from a racial perspective, while the GLAD (GLBTQ Legal Advocates and Defenders) organization has adapted it to measure the presence of LGBT collectives in movies. As the journalist Neda Ulaby explains in an interview for NPR, the test is useful because "it articulates something often missing in popular culture: not the number of women we see on screen, but the depth of their stories, and the range of their concerns" (Ulaby 2008).

When it comes to bertsolaritza, too, we can substitute the term "screen" for that of "stage" or "public space." Therefore, on the one hand the test will help to measure the public presence of women and, on the other, to visualize the depth of their stories and the range of their concerns. However, it will not include sessions that were expressly feminist, because we will not examine the discourse that is being constructed.

There is something in bertsolaritza does, though, that distinguishes it from fiction: in developing roles and characters, normally it reflects its point of view or opinion too. For that reason, when it comes to applying the Bechdel-Wallace test, it will be done in two dimensions:

> In-person: in a session in which more than one person was considered a woman socially, did at least two women converse with each other in bertsos and did they talk about something else besides a man (about their own experiences)?

> Portrayed: if at least two women characters were portrayed in a set of bertsos, did they converse with each other and did they talk about something else besides a man?

It is important to apply the two dimensions as complimentary, because one must bear in mind that, if one seeks to analyze how women's voices have been portrayed in bertsolaritza, for many years men took on the role in order to fulfill that task. Thus, seeing the influence that women taking to the stage has had, it is essential to address them both in-person and as portrayed. Moreover, as regards adding perspective, we must take into account that bertsolaritza has at specific moments played a role as a mirror of Basque society; and, until recently, men's voices have functioned as a replacement for half of that society. An analysis of the in-person portrayal of women alone would hide the voice and themes given to women as roles; on the contrary, taking just the portrayals would distort the public presence of women.

Defining the Samples

The decision was made to apply the methodology summarized above to the main sessions since the mid-1980s. The samples have been taken from bertso championship finals and bertso days during that period, and the bertso day has been held since 1968 (even though its format has evolved over the years). But the period would be too long for the study and as championships have mostly been addressed it would lead to variability by provinces. Thus, the 1986 National Championship was chosen as a starting point.

Since 1935, the National Bertsolari Championship has been the main showcase for bertsogintza, although it has experienced several changes along the way. Since 1982 it has been held every four years, and 1986 marks a watershed year as that was when the Association of Friends of Bertsolaritza began organizing the event. Consequently, one could say that since the National Championship took on its present-day form, we see this date as marking a rational starting point, being similar to the championship we know today, because the changes among bertsolaris and within bertsogintza will stand out in that stable structure.

It has been mentioned that the National Championship is the main showcase for bertsolaritza, and not in vain. As well as being the best attended sessions, they also receive the most media attention; thus, one could say that they are spaces in which the symbolic values of bertsolaritza are nourished.

For example, two journalists interpreted the symbolic meaning of the 2017 final in the following ways: "a cultural consensus has been decided, from instituting a standard language to that of establishing sociocultural values. In sum, it has been decided which are the common willows of a community's self-identification and self-recognition" (Eskisabel 2017). Along the same lines, the writer and journalist Kattalin Miner clarifies that in the National Championship, from the decision of "who creates bertsos alongside you," a lot of remarkable topics were addressed in the bertsos:

> Because we decide what culture is. Because we decide what speaking Basque is or how it should be. We decide and we establish which bertso activity will prevail. What it is to create bertsos. What is beautiful, and what is an essay on beauty . . . What worldview is appreciated. What makes the Basque Country and the world. What the girls who came this year were like. What are today's social topics. What politics is and what it is not. What humor is, what we can laugh at and what we cannot (even if we don't raise

a laugh). . . . What fiction is and what it is to sing on the basis of one's own selection. Who replaces us culturally. . . . What to bring to the table and what to leave behind (Miner 2017).

Clearly, then, the National Championship final sessions, as well as being very intense moments, are very important and prompt great skills. As a result, one could say that the way women are portrayed there influences society as a whole. It is not the most accurate guide to everyday bertsolaritza, but it is for most people a momentary picture that captures bertsogintza every four years.

That is what the bertsolari Jon Sarasua contends; specifically that it was the championship that encouraged the journal *Oral Tradition* to dedicate a special edition to bertsogintza. In particular, he writes that championship finals fulfill two kinds of function when considering bertsolaritza in recent decades: "On the one hand, they have attracted media and social attention (when they became a top-level event in the Basque Country); on the other hand, they have supported quality production by bertsolaris" (Sarasua 2007, 35).

The expert in orality John Miles Foley (one of the founders of *Oral Tradition*) also got to know bertsogintza first-hand by means of the championship. Later, he had the opportunity to understand it in more depth and he was able to see that the championship was just one more variant; nevertheless, he underscores the contribution of the championship to the oral movement as a whole. Specifically, it "is simply doing what oral poetry always does: it works on behalf of society, on behalf of ethnic and community values, as an adaptive mechanism for negotiating the world. In a real sense bertsolaritza is the pulse of Basque culture, an index of what it means to be Basque—past, present, and future" (Foley 2007, 11).

Another important annual date and showcase for bertsolaritza is the Bertso Day.[4] The first Bertsolari Day (it had this title until 1995) was held in 1968 and it celebrated the champion that year, Manuel Olaizola or "Uztapide." When it was founded, the Associa-

---

4   See "Bertso eguna," at the Euskal Herriko Bertsozale Elkartea (Association of Friends of Bertsolaritza) website: https://www.bertsozale.eus/eu/bertso-eguna.

tion of Friends of Bertsolaritza took over the organization of the
Bertsolari and Bertso Days. Since 1987, then, this association has
been in charge of running and managing the event.

In the change of name from Bertsolari to Bertso Day, the orga-
nizational model also changed: it ceased to be a celebration or tribute
and became an event designed to take a look at current bertsogintza.
As the Association of Friends of Bertsolaritza itself states, "new
goals were established: to reflect the changes in contemporary bert-
sogintza, to experiment, to get to know other experiences . . . Thus,
attempts have been made to seek a balance between improvised
creation and more prepared ways of appearing on stage."

The Bertso Day, then, is a very interesting feature of the sample
because it attempts to be an annual showcase for bertsogintza.
Therefore, it acts as a catalyst for the changes that, little by little,
bertsolaritza develops and helps others come into public view.

In sum, the sample is made up of: the final of the National
Bertsolaritza Championships, the provincial championship finals,
and the Bertso Days from 1986 onward. It can offer quite a broad
picture in order to describe the presence and development of women's
voices on the basis of the Bechdel test, because, as noted, as well
as noting this presence in the main public arenas of bertsogintza,
what emerges there also has social and symbolic meaning.

Besides those championship finals, there is another reason for
including the Bertso Days: the thing is, in order to be able to add
their voices to the sessions we will study, championship participants
must pass a qualification process. In the Bertso Days, however, just
as in other public performances, participants are invited to take
part by the organizers. In that sense, in examining the Bertso Day,
a simple choice on the part of the association is enough in order to
alter the in-person dimension of our test. In championship finals,
however, the whole structure is influential and changes need a longer
time-frame to see this.

The methodology designed will allow us to analyze those two
factors, and as the foundations of the performances in that time
period since the mid-1980s have been quite stable, for the most

part the development we can find will be according to the context or the bertsolaris. In other words, over the years it has been found that the factor that has most changed has been the bertsolaris and the content, because those are the objectives.

Results

In order to study how women's voices are represented, not many have observed how many voices have been those of women bertsolaris in the main performances. In the final analysis, the primary material that can reflect women's voices, with being dependent on the roles or situations suggested by theme prompters, are the women.

Within the tradition noted in the introduction, the means for women bertsolaris to take the stage are conditioned by social factors that are woven into the social and personal space (or lack of space) that the structure of societytabla assigns women. It is beyond the scope of this study, but if we were to just study National Championship finals, it would be worth looking at the number of women and men that have taken part on the way to qualifying for these.

Table 1. The Number of Women in Championships

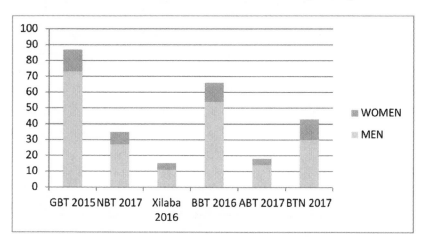

Among the bertsolaris that took part in the provincial championships, only those in first place qualified for the National Bertsolari

Championship (the quota for each province is different). And of the forty-three bertsolaris that took part in the National Bertsolari Championship, too, only eight qualified for the final, but as the previous champion also qualifies automatically, the rest compete for seven places.

It is worth bearing in mind, moreover, that in championships one single judging and operational structure conditions that classification. Moreover, the choice of an organizer that calls on bertsolaris to perform in a normal public setting is very different from that of the Association of Friends of Bertsolaritza organizing committee for the Bertso Days.

Table 2 shows the participants in National Bertsolari Championship finals that were also part of that year's Bertso Day: specifically, the first table shows the number of women and men that took part in National Bertsolari Championship finals between 1986 and 2017; while the second shows how many of those that took part in those finals also sang on the Bertso Day that year.

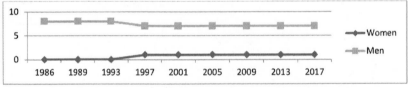

National Championship finals 1986–2017

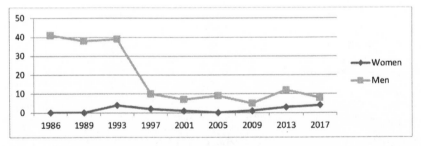

Table 2. The Number of Women in the Sample

*Bertso Egunak

As regards the Bertso Days, from 1995 onward, when there was a change of name from Bertsolari to Bertso day and a change in the objectives of the event, this change is reflected clearly in the overall number of bertsolaris. Looking at the National Championship, besides the initial drawing nearer of the two lines (representing women and men) in 1997, it is also striking that this does not happen thereafter. That means that there is no session in the National Championship that meets the Bechdel-Wallace test, outside the portrayal dimension. Because the existence of just one woman means that a conversation between two or more is impossible in the in-person dimension.

The Bertso Day lines draw clearly much closer together since less bertsolaris were chosen. Among all the bertsolaris that took part in championships we see a lot less women in the first table and if we were to place that in proportion it would be a lot more understandable. More than bertsolaritza, this is a reflection of society, its function (returning to Foley); it is speaking in the name of society and Basque culture, insofar that it is oral poetry. That being the case, the Bertso Day does not represent half of Basque culture, nor as we will see does it speak for that half, its role, or its situation.

In Table 3 we see if all the samples (National Bertsolari Championship and provincial finals as well as the main Bertso Day sessions) meet the norms of the test, both as regards the in-person and portrayal dimensions:

An initial look reveals that very few major sessions pass the test. Nowadays, just looking at championships, while there are fifty-five women bertsolaris, among those that have appeared in the main public spaces, as regards the in-person dimension only fifteen sessions meet the norms of the Bechdel-Wallace test. Out of 107 sessions, at least two women were on stage, conversing with one another, and about something else besides men, in fifteen of those. If we consider the portrayal dimension, thirty-one sessions meet the norms. That means that, in the roles assigned bertsolaris or when non-gender specific roles were given to women bertsolaris by the themes set, there were thirty-one bertso recitals among women without any defined relationships to men.

Table 3. Bechdel Test 1986 - 2001

Legend: ■ = Passed the Bechdel test · ▨ = Did not pass the Bechdel test · x = No data to apply the test

Year		B.E.	B.T.	G.T.	Xi	T.N.	A.T.	N.T.
1986	Perso	▨						
	Role	▨						
1987	Perso	▨						
	Role	▨						
1988	Perso	▨						
	Role	■						
1989	Perso	x				▨		
	Role	x				■		
1990	Perso	x						
	Role	x						
1991	Perso	x		▨				
	Role	x		■				
1992	Perso	▨						
	Role	▨						
1993	Perso	■				▨		
	Role	■				■		
1994	Perso	▨						■
	Role	▨						■
1995	Perso	▨		■				■
	Role	▨		■				■
1996	Perso	▨						▨
	Role	▨						▨
1997	Perso	■				■		x
	Role	■				■		x
1998	Perso	▨						▨
	Role	▨						▨
1999	Perso	x		▨				x
	Role	x		■				x
2000	Perso	▨	▨					x
	Role	▨	▨					x
2001	Perso	▨				▨		▨
	Role	▨						▨

■ Passed the Bechdel test.
▨ Did not pass the Bechdel test
x No data to apply the test

Table 3. Bechdel Test 2002 - 2017

		B.E.	B.T.	G.T.	Xi	T.N.	A.T.	N.T.
2002	Perso							
	Role							
2003	Perso							
	Role							
2004	Perso							
	Role							
2005	Perso							
	Role							
2006	Perso							
	Role							
2007	Perso							
	Role							
2008	Perso							
	Role							
2009	Perso							
	Role							
2010	Perso							
	Role							
2011	Perso							
	Role							
2012	Perso							
	Role							
2013	Perso							
	Role							
2014	Perso							
	Role							
2015	Perso							
	Role							
2016	Perso							
	Role							
2017	Perso							
	Role							

B.E. BERTSO EGUNA (every-year 'bertso day')
B.T. BIZKAIKO TXAPELKETA (regional campionship of Bizkaia)
G.T. GIPUZKOAKO TXAPELKETA (regional championship of Gipuzkoa)
Xi   XILABA (regional championship among Zuberoa,Lower Navarre and Lapurdi)
T.N. TXAPELKETA NAGUSIA (National bertsolaris championship)
A.T. ARABAKO TXAPELKETA (regional championship of Araba)
N.T. NAFARROAKO TXAPELKETA (regional championship of Navarre)

Female roles were portrayed by sessions made up just of men, but it was more usual to ask women to do so in the sessions in which they appeared. To cite some examples, in the 1986 National Bertsolari Championship the theme set for the individual three-verse session was the following: "Three bertsos to a nun that is working very silently up there in the retirement home at this very moment."[5] The phrase "very silently" is quite an appropriate metaphor for this chapter. At the same championship, another bertsolari was given the following topic: "One Sunday morning you get out of bed at eleven and when you go into the kitchen you see your old mom farting while she's making lunch." These are just two simple examples, but besides making a woman the object of the discourse, the spaces and tasks they portray is also important.

Instead of defining a man, most of the other topics are made up of assigning the roles of "wife" or "daughter" to the other bertsolari:[6] "You, Andoni Egaña, are retired and on a good pension, but you intend to go into a retirement home or a nursing home. You, Sarasua, his daughter, want him to stay at home." Yet as the chronogram proceeds, more defined and profound female roles are offered, asking for women's perspectives about many topics.

One striking change was assigning roles without specifying gender. In the 1980s and 1990s, for every topic, the words "you're a couple" were always followed by the specification that "A is the girl" and "B is the boy." Now on hearing the word "couple" it is more typical for the individual to choose the gender they think appropriate for the role (so long as they do not want to do a specific job of changing gender). For example, at the final of the 2016 Bizkaia Bertsolari Championship,[7] the following theme was set: "Miren, Nerea came from Bolivia to the Basque Country and you met each other here. You have a four-year-old daughter. Nerea's family don't know your daughter. During the winter break you'll go to Bolivia for the first time." One of the characters was Bolivian, they were a couple, and it was the turn of two women, that is, it was about a gay couple. That

---

5   National Bertsolari Championship, final, Donostia, March 23, 1986.
6   Ibid.
7   Bizkaia Bertsolari Championship, final, Bilbo, December 17, 2016.

implied a worrying focus, for instead of the issue just being about the child, the journey also implied doubts about what may happen if their relationship was not acknowledged in Bolivia.

Miren Amuriza
hemen tratetan zaitut
modu xamurrean
ta muxuka al zaitzaket
beraien aurrean?

Can I treat you
in the same affectionate way as here
and kiss you
in front of them?

And the round of bertsos finished in the following way:

Nerea Ibarzabal
asko maite zaitut ta
gora "Bollivia"
I love you so much
and long live Bolivia!

In championships chance decrees who will sing on what topic. In festivals, however, the theme prompter can decide who gets a situation, topic, or character. In such situations, the theme prompter usually attaches an intention to the topic, or adapts the topic for the character; or even thinks it up for them too. That is the case, precisely, of the Bertso Day.

This festivals met the norms, in both dimensions, of the Bechdel-Wallace text for the first time in 1993 and that fact in itself became the theme for three women bertsolaris: "Three girls for the first time at the Bertsolari Day."[8] Those young bertsolaris were being called on to reflect, in some way, on that experience. They took the opportunity, emphasizing that they had been called on finally and recalling that this would have been unthinkable "twenty years ago." However, the "anecdote" of the performance was its critical role and this is how it ended:

---

8   Bertsolari Day, Donostia, January 24, 1993.

Maialen Lujanbio

*Lehenago hauek osatzen zuten
bertso munduko bizitza
beraiena zen irakaskuntza
ta beraiena zen hitza.*

Those that came before established
the life of the bertso world
the teaching was theirs
and the word was theirs.

Estitxu Arozena

*Emakumeok mikrofonoan
jaso izan dugu burla
gaur ere batzuk haserre daude
ezin dute disimula.*

*Ni ziur nago egunen baten
erakutsiko dugula
bertsolaritzak barrabilekin
zerikusirik ez dula!*

We women at the microphone
have been ridiculed
even today some are angry
they can't hide it.
I'm sure that one day
we'll show that
bertsolaritza has nothing
to do with balls!

In the same session the following topic was given to six male bert-solaris: "You are six single girls celebrating a bachelorette party." In all likelihood, this topic would have been addressed quite differently had women been chosen to take the stage.

Some years later, the goal of the 2014 Bertsolari Day was to develop a gender perspective and a special effort was made throughout the day as well as in the main festival to undertake gender work.

That session, obviously, met the norms of the test (and in a parallel universe, if we were to apply the Bechdel-Wallace test to measure the presence of men in that session, that would also pass). To choose one significant round of bertsos, I will select that of Rosi Lazkano, Onintza Enbeita, and Saioa Alkaiza,[9] because there a female voice appeared that is not usually portrayed: they addressed women's sexuality and menstruation, from three different stages in women's lives (around twenty years old, thirty-five to forty years old, and over fifty).

Rosi Lazkano
beraz ez naiz hasiko saltoka
armairuraino igota
eztarritik ta beste hortatik
nahiko sekoa nago ta
so I won't start jumping around
up on top of the closet
because my throat and everything else
is quite dry

Onintza Enbeita
Nire alua urgente dago
beste esku bat eskatzen
My vagina is urgent
demanding another hand

One does not often hear, within the public bertso arena, women over fifty years old and there is rarely a specific space to develop such a specific topic based on such understanding. Singing to women about sexuality or portraying women's sex is one thing; but it is quite another groundbreaking thing, compared to traditional portrayals, to say one is "dry" or indirectly cite masturbation. The Bechdel-Wallace test, as noted, does not register whether a show is feminist or not, but it does offer a starting point on which to base a discussion.

---

9   Bertso Day, Donostia, 2014. The session can be seen at https://bertsoa.eus/bertsoak/10998-enbeita-lazkano-eta-alkaiza-dibanean.

Discussion

Starting with those most recent examples, in the event of having
two or more women communicating about something else besides
a man, one can hear things that would not be sung by others. There
are discourses that cannot be carried out by some replacements; and
if it acts in the name of society, bertsolaritza is also responsible for
creating spaces like that. The change is taking is taking place in public
spaces, even though, looking at the main championships, clearly in
most sessions the aforementioned norms are not met.

As regards representation, an evolution is slowly coming into view.
Women, to put it succinctly, went from being a subject of bertsos
to being represented in the mouths of men; they were originally
conceived in terms of their relationship to men and subsequently
became a more general topic. Once women started appearing in
public, however, they went from being signs to being signifiers
and those roles have been developed more profoundly and more
broadly through practice. There is still a long way to go to bring
those two lines in the tables together, but more and more women
are setting out on the path. As Andoni Egaña sang in the farewell
bertso at the 1997 final:

> bertsolaritza aurrera doa
> *emakumeen harira*
> *82ko Txapelketari*
> *jarri gaitezen begira*
> *orduan gaitzat hartzen genitun*
> *ta orain eurak gai dira.*

> bertsolaritza is forging ahead
> following the direction of women.
> Just take a look at
> the 82 championship.
> Then we looked at them badly,
> and now they're more than capable.

Furthermore, one must remember that if one session passes the test it does not mean that there is a good gender equality model. It does not mean that women's roles are well done, necessary, real, or profound; just that they exist and that is all. Systematically studying many sessions, though, a more gendered tendency in bertsolaritza may emerge; and that may help to establish the direction of future work that needs to be done.

The work does not just come out of the mouth of the bertsolari, because in the sessions described here one can see that the organizer, the judging structure, and the theme prompters play a key role in influencing the discourse. Non-gender specific themes, for example, have brought with them a change in many sessions and while they are not typical on an everyday basis, looking at sessions since the mid-1980s one sees that this small nuance has helped to reflect other kinds of family models and relationships.

Returning to the research questions, as regards the presence of women's voices one could say that the sessions that did not meet the norms of the test represent a significant majority and consequently, the female voice was either not represented, or, when it was represented, that in most cases it was represented in the context of relationships with men. Passing the test in representations of some sessions in which there were not two or more women on stage demonstrates that men sang in the character of women in those sessions. Thus, the presence of women's voices was delimited and often represented by men.

Turning to the second question, the arrival of women in public spaces has changed the way of representing women in bertsolaritza: from singing to a woman (the object of a bertso) to singing in the role of a woman; from the woman just appearing in the role of "wife" to more specific reflections on and preoccupations about the situation experienced by a wife; from the preoccupations that may be experienced by a wife to addressing other kinds of general concerns (about social as well as political topics); and, finally, to defining non-gender roles (in cases in which, specifically, that is not the objective).

In the mid-1980s, in order to represent women's voices, in order to portray those characters, on stage, bertsolaritza was able to make the effort from its function as a mirror of society. There is a difference, however, between the interpretation, humor, and discourse of a man and what a woman may do. Even so, putting a woman on stage is not, in itself, equivalent to representing women's voices. One could make an important contribution in order to create a discourse, even though one cannot ask just one bertsolari to represent half of society. Experiences are variable and subjective, and so portraying more characters means wider choices in order to reveal their nuances, cracks, and crevices.

If we understand the stage as a powerful in-person space, we understand the concept of hegemony in slightly wider terms, and we will realize that, in gender terms, it is not the only fissure. Along the same lines, the change brought about by women taking to public spaces can help us understand how such stage diversity offers a wider choice in order to represent society.

Adapting slightly what T. J. Jackson Lears (1985, 569) observes about film,[10] bertsolaritza can be the key to the persistence of gender inequality in society; and that is part of the concept of cultural hegemony. Keys have the ability to both open and close, however, and what serves to help gender inequality persist can, if turned the other way, also help construct gender equality.

Bibliography

Agarwal, Apoorv, Jiehan Zheng, Kamath, Shruti Vasanth Kamath, Sriram Balasubramanian, and Shirin Ann Dey. 2015. "Key Female Characters in Film Have More to Talk About Besides Men: Automating the Bechdel Test." In *Human Language Technologies: The 2015 Annual Conference of the North American Chapter of the ACL.* Proceedings of the Conference. N.p.: Association

---

10   The original sentence is: "The centralized nature of movies plays a key role in the persistence of gender inequality in a society, which is part of the concept of cultural hegemony."

for Computational Linguistics. At https://pdfs.semanticschol-ar.org/dfaf/97f709be25faceb91e218964bd288a138e0e.pdf (last accessed February 22, 2018).

Agirre, Lorea. 2010. "Zapia eta txapela. Emakume bertsolariak tradizioarekin negoziatzen eta eredu berria sortzen. Negoziazioak eta disonantziak: mututasunetik emulaziora, eta emulaziotik ahots propiora." Master's Thesis, Arrasate: HUHEZI. At file:///C:/Users/cjw74/Downloads/2010%20Lorea%20Agirrezapia%20eta%20txapela.pdf (last accessed February 22, 2018).

Ardener, Edwin, and Shirley Ardener. 1975. *Perceiving Women*. London: J.M. Dent & Sons Ltd.

Eizagirre, Estitxu. 2014. *Bidea urratu duten bertsoak*. Lasarte-Oria: Argia and Emakundea.

Eskisabel, Idurre. 2017. "Gure inurri horiek." *Berria*, December 23. At https://www.berria.eus/paperekoa/1955/026/001/2017-12-23/txapelketa_gure_inurritegi_hori.htm (last accessed February 16, 2018).

Foley, John Miles. 2007. "Basque Oral Poetry Championship." *Oral Tradition* 22, no. 2: 3–11.

Garcia, David, Ingmar Weber, and , Venkata Rama Kiran Garimella. 2014. "Gender Asymmetries in Reality and Fiction: The Bechdel Test of Social Media." *Proceedings of the Eighth International Conference on Weblogs and Social Media*. ICWSM 2014. N.p.: AAAI Press.

Garzia, Joxerra, Jon Sarasua, and Andoni Egaña. 2001. *The Art of Bertsolaritza: Improvised Basque Verse Singing*. Donostia: Bertsozale Elkartea.

Hickey, Walt. 2014. "The Dollar-And-Cents Case Against Hollywood's Exclusion of Women." *FiveThirtyEight*. ABC News, April 1. At https://fivethirtyeight.com/features/the-dollar-and-cents-case-against-hollywoods-exclusion-of-women/ (last accessed February 18, 2018).

Labaka, Ane. 2017. Interview with Patxi Etxeberria for the online jour-
nal *bertsoa*, June 29. At https://bertsoa.eus/albisteak/6450-nire-
arreba-ere-bertsolari-izango-zen-seguruena-aukera-izan-balu
(last accessed January 19, 2018).

Larrañaga, Carmen 1994. "Bertsolarismo: habitat de la masculinidad."
Bitarte 4: 29–51.

———. 1995. "Bertsolarismo: una tradición transitada por el género-
sexo." *Vasconia. Cuadernos de historia-geografía* 23: 405–25.

———. 1997. "Del bertsolarismo silenciado." *Jentilbaratz* 6: 57–73.

Lawrence, K. Faith. 2011. "SPARQLing Conversation: Automating
The Bechdel–Wallace Test." Paper presented at the Narrative
and Hypertext Workshop, Hypertext. At http://nht.ecs.soton.
ac.uk/2011/papers/12-flawrence.pdf (last accessed January 12,
2018).

Lears, T. J. Jackson. 1985. "The Concept of Cultural Hegemony:
Problems and Possibilities." *American Historical Review* 90, no. 3:
567–93.

Lemonauria, Pedro. 1837. *Ensayo crítico sobre las leyes constitucionales de
Vizcaya*. Bilbao: Delmas.

Miner, Kattalin 2017. "Bazterren aroa behingoz." *Argia*, December
19. At http://www.argia.eus/albistea/bazterren-aroa-behingoz
(last accessed February 16, 2018).

San Sebastian, Xabino, Inazio Usarralde, and Nikolas Zeberio. 2002.
Gai-jartzailearen eskuliburua. Donostia: Euskal Herriko Bertso-
zale Elkartea.

Sarasua, Jon. 2007. "Social Features Of Bertsolaritza." *Oral Tradition*
22, no. 2: 33–46.

Sharma, Versha, and Hanna Sender. 2014. "Hollywood Movies With
Strong Female Roles Make More Money". *Vocativ*, January 2.
At http://www.vocativ.com/culture/celebrity/hollywood-mov-
ies-strong-female-roles-make-money/ (last accessed January
12, 2018).

Snow, Georgia 2015. "Theatre gets its own Bechdel Test". *The Stage*, November 30. https://www.thestage.co.uk/news/2015/theatre-gets-its-own-bechdel-test/ (last accessed January 7, 2018).

Ulaby, Neda. 2008. "The 'Bechdel Rule,' Defining Pop-Culture Character." *All Things Considered*, NPR, September 2. At https://www.npr.org/templates/transcript/transcript.php?storyId=94202522.

Woolf, Virginia. 1929. *A Room of One's Own*. Web edition published by eBooks@Adelaide, the University of Adelaide Library, University of Adelaide.

Data Sources

Xenpelar Dokumentazio Zentroa (http://bdb.bertsozale.eus/web/bertsoa/bilaketa).

Mintzola Ahozko Lantegia (https://www.mintzola.eus/eu).

EITB:

Hitzetik hortzera (http://www.eitb.eus/eu/telebista/programak/hitzetik-hortzera/).

Bertsoaren aldagela (http://www.eitb.tv/eu/bideoa/hitzetik-hortzera-bertsolari-txapelketa-nagusia-2013/4104744476001/4090123454001/bertsoaren-aldagelan/)

Bertso plaza digitala (www.bertsoa.eus).

CHAPTER 3

As the Tree Grows, the Bark Cracks

Maialen Lujanbio

The Evolution of Bertsolaritza
from 1975 to the Present:
Bertso Schools and the Initiation of Women

"There have always been female improvised *bertsolaris*," I say quite confidently, even though I do not know exactly when they started to sing, or how, or where. Actually, even in the absence of historical proof, through what some may consider a naive reading of things, we could argue that since ours has always been *kantatzen duen herria*—the country that sings—we can naturally assume that it was not just half of the country that did the singing. Besides, if we take into account that the transmission of Euskara (the Basque language) was mostly a female endeavor, and that language transmission is carried out through song too, and that songs carry sounds and melodies, and melodies and sounds carry affection, then we can safely conclude that women have "always" sung. And quite probably improvised too, in the process.

In any case, beyond issues of historical evidence or naivety, we have archival, written proof that women have been singing bertsos since at least as far back as 1432.

The names of celebrated bertsolaris down to twenty-first century have mostly been male. In contrast, we have often heard, from our older relatives, comments like: "in our family, it was mom who sung bertsos!" or "the best bertsolri in this family was always our aunt." If this was the case until recently, we can safely assume that things were like this before too. A different issue is that we barely received any news of female bertsolaris , for social and political reasons. Women (who sang bertsos) did not have any opportunities to do so in public spaces—not in town squares, not in festivals, and not in front of audiences. However, bertsolari women did exist, and they did sing.

Although it has been historically difficult to sing in the public space of the town square while being a female, it has not been particularly easy to be a Basque speaker there either. For the last one hundred years, French has been imposed infamously in the Northern Basque Country, while Euskara was grievously and slowly forgotten. The Southern Basque Country suffered under Franco's dictatorship from 1939 to 1975, and his fascist regime forbade and decimated the Basque language and culture during those years.

It took almost forty years to get through the dark tunnel of Francoism in the Southern Basque Country, and we can date the origins of modern *bertsolaritza* precisely to the end of that time. Today, when forty more years have passed since the end of Francoism, we can look back and contemplate the road we have traveled since then: the events that have caused bertsolaritza to become a powerful art form and, especially, the key elements that explain the space women have carved out for themselves in bertsolaritza. "'In Hernani, in 1975, you were setting subjects for Lasarte and Lazkao Txiki to sing about. At the time, did you believe that they were destined to be the last bertsolaris?' 'Yes. Think of what the previous forty years had been like: the total oppression of Euskara, its prohibition . . . The oldest bertsolaris were dying, and we didn't have a formula to create new ones'."[1]

The Way Out of the Tunnel

In the words of Juanjo Uria, founder of the first bertso school in Hernani, "Those who were concerned with the situation regarding Basque cultural activity wanted to do something about the Basque language, about culture in Basque... one of the components in that movement was bertsolaritza."[2] The Basque language and culture had to build themselves up from nothing. The *ikastolas*, or Basque-language schools, were operational again (before, and throughout the nineteenth and twentieth centuries, a number of isolated and clandestine ikastolas existed both in the Northern and in the Southern Basque Country), and they went on to proliferate, and go from strength to strength in the 1960s and 1970s. There can be no doubt that the language and culture transmission project ignited by those activists went on to become the main foundation of what would eventually become the Basque-speaking Basque Country: "Some bertso schools began in ikastolas. For example, the ikastola in Zumaia was the first to offer bertsolaritza classes during normal tuition hours, starting in 1975. Many other bertso schools were born as a consequence of lectures given by Xabier Amuriza. The first one of those was the bertso school in Santutxu" ("Bertso eskolek 25 urte" 2018).

> I too was a child of the ikastola. Euskara is my mother tongue, I spoke it at home. My entire education was carried out in Basque, from kindergarten to university. For as long as I can remember, I have loved the Basque language, have felt a burning for it. No one ever imposed that on me or explicitly communicated that to me. It was just something I felt. Euskara was me. Is me. I am Euskara.

1   Juanjo Uria, interview by Edu Lartzanguren, *Berria*, December 24, 2017.
2   Juanjo Uria, quoted in "Bertso eskolek 25 urte," *Argia*, February 24, 2018.

"We are (in) Basque." The basic shared feeling of those of us who dwell in the world of bertsolaritza can be reduced to this sentence. Because there is no bertsolaritza without the Basque language; the existence of the two has always been, and will be, inextricably linked. According to a bertso by Iñaki Eizmendi, otherwise known as Basarri:

"Gure lurrean guk eztaukagu/	"Tell me why we should,
zertan egon buruz bera/	in our own land
	be sad and hang our heads low.
Une honetan aitor dezagun:	Right this moment, let's make a plan:
bagera edo ez gera!/	come on: are we or are we not now!
Bertsolaritza bizi dan arte/	If we keep bertsolaritza alive
biziko baita euskera."	you know Euskara will follow."[3]

Bertsolaris have always been greatly concerned with the state of Euskara. In the 1980s, the possibility that the Basque language might disappear was very real and very present. The risk was evident. While it was plausible that the ikastolas might help strengthen the Basque language, it was harder to believe that bertsolaritza might gain strength through schools. Very few people back then defended the idea of teaching bertsolaritza at schools. Until then, in the Basque imagination, people were born bertsolaris. Not everyone could be one. Only a few were born with that special gift for improvisation (and, as luck would have it, those few were all men). For Uria, "Back then everybody said: 'a bertsolari can only be born with the gift'. And that meant that bertsolaritza wasn't something that could be learned, and we internalized that message completely. But then Amuriza happened, and he said: 'Who says bertsolaritza can't be taught?' We owe him the continuity of the art."[4]

3   Iñaki Eizmendi, "Basarri," December 18, 1989, Bertsolaritza Database (hereafter BDB), Xenpelar Dokumentazio Zentroa, Andoain.
4   Juanjo Uria, interview by Edu Lartzanguren, *Berria*, December 24, 2017.

The Birth of Bertso Schools

We are indebted to the great bertsolari Xabier Amuriza, among other things, for the idea of creating and expanding bertso schools. He created the methodology and the materials to make teaching bertsolaritza a possibility and a social endeavor. For example, he wrote *Zu ere bertsolari* (You too can be a bertsolari, 1982) and *Hiztegi errimatua* (The rhyming dictionary, 1997). He was a great bertsolari who, instead of keeping and *preserving* his knowledge for himself, had the generosity and foresight to pass it on to others.

> The initial objective of some of the bertso schools was to improve students' Basque language levels. For some others, the objective was to develop the population's taste for bertsolaritza, and only a few of them had the audacity to conceive the possibility of creating bertsolaris. We believed in education, and envisioned it as a challenge: we will become and will create bertsolaris. Our biggest hope was to prove that this was possible. We even had nonnative Basque speakers in our bertso schools, and we showed that even they could learn to sing bertsos ("Bertso eskolek 25 urte" 2018).

The linguistic and cultural situation was so dire, it was imperative to take risks. There was almost nothing left to lose. The fight for survival made committed lovers of the Basque language and bertsolaritza act with generosity of mind and spirit. Since it was not a given that transmission would take place as a "natural" process, they designed a strategy for transmission. Both for the ikastolas and for the bertso schools.

> Artifice vs. naturalness: the Basque Country was an invention; the politicized Basque Country, as a nation. The country's culture became a nation's culture. The home became the square. And if it hadn't been invented, it would have been lost. That is the objective of ideology: to build a society. To deliberately build a society, knowing

what's wanted. If the intent is to exercise transmission in postmodern conditions, then it will necessarily have to be carried out artificially.[5]

It happened with postmodernity and with modernity: both times they invented "bertso school." And invent it they did!

Hindered, Therefore progressive

Besides being a visionary, Xabier Amuriza was incredibly generous with his successors. A posteriori, we haver learned that his acts of transmission, which seemed such "natural" behavior at the time, do not always happen so easily. Having come into contact with other improvisational cultural phenomena (in South America, for example), we came to realize that although many other improvisational forms were also in similarly dire situations, that kind of transmission did not take place. Why though? The answer might be the fight for survival. Something that those dwelling in hegemonic languages did not feel, because there was no immediate risk. The survival of their language was guaranteed—even if their art form was left to die. We, on the other hand, the Basques, have a constant sense of life or death regarding our country and our language. We fear losing something that is ours, or, rather, something that we are, and it is most likely the awareness of the risk of that loss has made Basque activist people so generous and progressive.

This is something that was imprinted into the pedagogical structures of the ikastolas and the mechanics created for the transmission of bertsolaritza. In the words of Joxerra Garzia, Jon Sarasua, and Andoni Egaña:

> So, bertsolaritza has had a remarkable trajectory of survival and adaptation in a small community, but it faces a serious challenge for the future. A challenge of survival as, in some areas, it is on the point of extinction and is seriously threatened by novel forms of cultural and linguis-

---

5   Eduardo Apodaka, "Hau koaderno bat zen," lecture, HUHEZI, Lanku, Mondragon Unibertsitatea, 2009.

tic uniformity. It is a challenge, nevertheless, which the wide spectrum of people who support the art are taking on more and more in the activist and entertaining sense of the term than in its negative or dramatic one (Garzia, Sarasua, and Egaña 2001, 36).

Bertso Schools: Undoing the Myths

Bertso schools were up and running; both in the ikastolas, with girls and boys; and with adults too, in towns and cities like Bilbao.

The first traditional myth that needed undoing was that one needed to be *born* a bertsolari. And undoing that first myth, of course, caused the next old myth to collapse as well: namely, that women did not do bertsolaritza.

Quite likely, female participation was a result of the open-mindedness required by any culture that is in a life-or-death situation. In other words, when you have little left to loose, inevitably the general attitude is one that embraces risk-taking. And since bertsolaritza was at risk of disappearing, it was everybody's job to save it, including women.

I was six or seven years old. I must have barely known what bertsolaritza was, but I remember how our teacher once told us that someone named Arantzazu Loidi had won first prize at the bertso school championship. Arantzazu Loidi, I did not realize at the time that her comment would be forever imprinted into my mind.

Without lessening the value of what came before, but always aiming for renewal, bertsolaritza has shown itself to be generous with the new generations. And that has proven to be one of the greatest reasons for its success.

Perhaps we do have something to teach the world after all.

What was the Bertso School?

The bertso school was an informal school in which we worked on developing our love of bertsolaritza. Almost anarchic. More like a group of friends, where people of all ages gathered together. It was a special habitat for young people who shared the same passion.

At the beginning, the aim of those teachers was to encourage the children to enjoy the world of bertsolaritza: we would sing old bertsos, and, through them, learned old melodies; we learned to appreciate the bertsolaris' use of language and their witty sayings, to internalize the internal logic of bertsolaritza bit by bit. We heard stories about old bertsolaris, Etxhaun's adventures, those of Bilintx, and so forth. There were no rules to any of it, the methodology was invented; the aim, pure enjoyment. After that, slowly, there would be exercises to train the children in bertsolaritza: metrics, melodies, rhymes, words, and, in the end, suddenly there would be song.

> I hardly knew anything about bertsolaritza. There was not much of that at home. When I joined the bertso school when I was ten or eleven I hardly even knew who Amuriza was. I did not know what a sung bertso was. I well remember the question always gnawing at me back then: "how do you know when a sung bertso is good?"

We used to waste hours of teaching. Having learned a few rudiments of bertso singing, young pupils would take it upon themselves to pass the knowledge on to the younger ones, and like this a chain of transmission was created, which encouraged attachment and a sense of teamwork.

We enjoyed ourselves and that, and only that, was the objective.

Bertso schools spread and proliferated all over the Basque Country. The foundations of the bertsolaritza of the future were being built.

But the 1980s was a very skeptical decade. The staunchest traditionalists would not accept that the bertsolaris that came out of those schools could ever be "real bertsolaris." Even though this precarious machinery for the reigniting of the bertsolaritza tradition had been assembled, there was no guarantee that the endeavor would bring results.

The bertso schools' bertsolari championship was created to encourage young children to improvise bertsos in public, and, in that same competition in which a girl called Arantzazu Loidi won the main prize, we also set foot on a stage for the first time to sing improvised bertsos to an audience.

We met up with kids from other bertso schools. We were rather "peculiar" young people, little girls and boys engaging in a pastime for "old people," preoccupied Euskara speakers, language lovers, song lovers; these were not the usual concerns of the girls and boys of our generation.

I say girls and boys, but it was mostly boys.

> While She was a Female Bertsolari,
> She did not Know the Joys and Sorrows
> of Being a Female Bertsolari
> When I was at the ikastola, the Basque school, I did not feel
> like a girl among boys, I just felt like a friend in a group of
> friends. I didn't feel "peculiar," although in the bertso-
> singing world they continuously reminded me of that fact.
> When we met with young people from other schools, team-
> work always seemed easier among the boys. Perhaps because
> of the age difference, most of the young boys acted mostly
> distant, cold and polite (too polite) toward me. It kind of felt
> like I was an acquaintance while they were pals. I felt that
> metaphorically as well as literally. But at the time I was not
> really conscious of this. The strangeness, the newness, the
> nervousness, everything was mixed up; and I managed to
> adapt. In the end, I was used to being in those spaces.
> I was always playing soccer with the boys during recess.
> (If you were better than average they'd let you play).

My debut took place in Hondarribia. In 1988. The year I entered the bertso schools' championship for the first time I was eleven years old and the only girl in a group of eleven tiny bertsolaris. The presenter introduced me as if I were a special surprise, saying something like: "and look at this, today we have a girl!"

Following the usual structure of a bertsolari performance, we would approach the microphone and hold our bodies very still and stiff and try to sing as powerfully as possible. The format was a given, and we had to adapt to it. The format, besides, did not only encompass form; subjects and perspectives were also very specific.

"Stand up Maialen," they called me to sing my first-ever improvised song in public, "these are your four rhymes: *Marino* / *Pino* / *Cubino* / *animo!*"

I was an eleven-year-old girl.

Marino, *Pino*, and *Cubino* were three cyclists taking part in the Tour of Spain cycling race. And I was supposed to know that.

> The room filled with tension.
> It is imprinted in my mind. In my skin.
> "What can she know about that."

Thinking back, it does not seem the most appropriate challenge for an eleven-year-old child (a girl at that), but apparently no one took that into account. It was a sports matter, a news matter, a man's matter—and therefore a matter of "general" interest.

But that's what bertsolaritza was like.

Karreran lehenegoa	*Well ahead, first on the race*
zijoan CUBINO	*leads our man CUBINO*
harek lehen atzetikan	*and who follows close behind*
zedukala PINO	*but ambitious PINO*
baina ero(r)i in ziran	*and look now hittin' the ground*
bera ta MARINO	*both him and MARINO*
Hala ta guztiz haiei	*but no matter, keep going*
milaka ANIMO!	*go on guys, GO, GO, GO!*

> I knew about it. I knew very well who those three cyclists
> were and what had happened in the previous day's race
> during the Tour of Spain.
> But the truth is,
> there is no reason why I should have known that.

In that same round, straight after me, they gave Unai Agirre the following four rhymes: *zazpi* / *noski* / *whiski* / *gaizki* (lucky / undoubtedly / whisky / badly).

Whisky. It does not seem like the most appropriate reference in the world for a twelve year old. But that is what bertsolaritza was: the mold was made to fit the measure of grown men.

What Was Bertsolaritza?

Bertso singing had its quirks. Its exchange codes, its way of relating things to one another, its witty ways, aesthetics, reasoning, humor. And all those things were passed down in the bertso schools, even if it was unconsciously; renewal through the power of repetition. For Mari Luz Esteban (2004, 9),

> Beyond their natural ability and training in bertso-singing, young pupils are educated in a set of bodily attitudes and techniques, which constitute the typical posture of a bertsolari, which—while allowing variations—requires that a person stands up straight, standing their ground, portraying in this way a fundamental value in Basque culture, which is the expression of "power" . . . In the case of bertsolaritza, this expression is not an expression of physical power . . . but rather it is a display of the ability to resist, to stand one's ground, to have "staying power."

That is what bertsolaritza was, an attitude based on sharp answers and the weight of reason, and, until someone proved the opposite at least, that was "the way" bertsos were sung: subjects were current to the times and the environment. The socially important ones: the political situation, our endangered Basque language; love relationships—defined very stereotypically and always from a man's perspective; family; the church; the farming world and farming work; sports; food and drink and partying. The context was masculine. The partying context: gastronomic societies and the endless meals in them (often, women were forbidden from entering gastronomic societies, exceptions being made only for female bertsolaris—for bertsolaris and for cleaners, of course). To eat and to drink were values in themselves in those gatherings—not wanting to eat anymore meant you somehow fell short. They would go late into the night. The atmosphere similar to that of a bar, or a rowdy show or a *fronton* court. The subjects of conversation were typically masculine: hunting, sports, politics, women. Their jokes and comments about women delivered as if you were not there. But you were there. Silent and invisible. Invisible or insignificant.

> I did not have to specially adapt to that habitat.
> Or maybe it is just that I knew how to adapt, I am not sure.
> I did not sense that the show of strength was a performance.
> It was my world too, those were my ways too.

Describing a female bertsolari, Esteban observes: "Arrate's is still a young body, still growing, but powerful, rotund, in one piece, and this shows it is rooted in Basque culture . . . a body that fits the corporeity of a bertsolari . . . but that simultaneously contains a challenge to the culture itself, from within itself" (ibid.).

In the bertso-singing/bertsolaris' world, we had to play by "their" rules. We did not know any other way. Be strong, respond.

Back then we would hear "that girl has some balls!" from expert men and know-alls, and such comments had to be understood as a sign of acceptance.

"I didn't mean to say that she's got balls to spare /

I meant that those with balls would happily go there...," someone else would sing, and there would be a chorus of laughter.

> I would laugh too.
> Nervous laughter, part-unconscious,
> part-I-prefer-not-to-notice. A different kind of laugh-
> ter. Complacent. A visitor's laughter, uneasy in their host's
> home. Did my lack of awareness allow me to move forward?
> Were those voices, those bodies, those attitudes,
> an unavoidable requirement to survive in that habitat?

At that time, it was unthinkable that a woman bertsolari displaying characteristics considered typically feminine—neat, groomed, carefully dressed—would perform in the bertso-singing public spaces of the Basque Country.

"Sermoiek eta neskatxen gonak	"Both a priests' sermon and a girls' skirt
behar dute alde gutxi	should share two commonalities
izan behar dute ahalik motzenak	they must always be very, very short,
ta ahalik gehien erakutsi."	and inspire, but also tease."

Bertsolaritza was like that.

Inside the Young Generation

But it was not only that.

For me, camaraderie has been essential in bertsolaritza. Actually, that is what bertso school is most of all: a group of friends who share something they love. I did not learn to sing bertsos in bertso school. Bertso-singing culture, the milieu of bertsolaris—those things had a greater influence.

I did not go to bertso school every week. The few times I did go, I would try very hard not to sing. Unlike the one in our school, the bertso school in our town felt like the true realm of bertsolaritza. It was traditional, filled with older men. It felt unfamiliar and it stressed me out, always forcing me try (too) hard. Thankfully, there were other young bertsolaris there. People who had other interests apart from the interests that are assumed a lover of bertsolaritza should have, who shared other social and cultural points of reference. People who were closer to my generation, in other words.

I needed that: friends who were not only bertsolaris or bertso aficionados, but who also shared (my) other concerns and desires.

> I think that that is what we, the young bertsolaris, found
> in what would eventually become "the young generation:"
> togetherness. That group was our salvation.

Unai Agirre and Jexux Mari Irazu in Hernani. Later, Jon Maia,
Iratxe Ibarra, Unai Iturriaga, Igor Elortza, Estitxu Arozena, Xabier
Silveira . . . we new young debutants in the world of bertsolaritza
soon felt a spontaneous sense of kinship, a sense of being part of
a generation and the budding conscience of a desire to infuse new
blood into the world of bertsolaritza.

What did that Generation Bring?

Besides starting to take part in the habitual bertsolaritza circuits,
"young improvised bertsolari sessions" slowly started to become
more and more common.

Before us, too, Amuriza first, and mostly Egaña and Sarasua later
on, had already started to develop new forms and ideas that went
beyond the "traditional" language of bertsolaritza. The Bertsolaritza
Association had just recently been created and one of its achieve-
ments was to get bertsolaritza recognized as a cultural movement.
Bertsolaritza was not just something that older men did when they
were drinking.

In the words of Garzia, Sarasua, and Egaña, "The bertsolaris,
and in general all those involved in the movement, have opted for
trying out new spaces and forms, for getting into television, for look-
ing for forms and dimensions hitherto unknown to bertsolaritza"
(Garzia, Sarasua, and Egaña 2001, 64).

Those little droplets of bertsolaritza renewal became rivulets,
and the rivulets, with the new generation, would become a wave. We
caught the wave, or maybe the wave caught us. Young bertsolaris
modernized and adapted bertsolaritza to their times. They introduced
new attitudes, aesthetics and subjects: drugs, alternative discourses
about love and sexual relationships, different cultural references,
different ways of singing, of using the language, and so on.

Bertsolaritza came to the city. It updated itself, thematically. In terms of form, artistic exercises started to proliferate, collaborations began to take place—with music, with other arts.

The band Negu Gorriak recorded its "bertso-hop" song using Egaña and Peñagarikano's bertsos and setting them to a hip-hop beat. It was a small revolution. Several bertsolaris took part in a farewell concert for the famed rock band Ertzainak and sang its verses. Bertsolaritza was beginning to acquire a new image.

It started inhabiting new spaces; places and sociological contexts that were unthinkable before: occupied buildings in which alternative communities lived, metal-heads' hangouts, for example. Young bertsolari boys and girls and what they brought into the art caused young male and female audiences to come and meet them in public. The whole ecosystem began to breathe new air.

Resistance to the New

That new generation brought renewal into the squares; and, of course, new things always provoke resistance. On the one hand, we was the generation that had learned the craft in bertso schools. We were not "natural" or "authentic" or "born bertsolaris." We would have to demonstrate that we were as good at bertsolaritza as those who came before us. On the other, our notions, our way with language, our humor, our singing styles, and our aesthetics were rejected by the more staunch Basque traditionalists; and, it goes without saying, the fact that women were engaged in bertsolaritza! "I will never get used to hearing women sing bertsos," we used to hear.

For some, we were (are?) not good enough bertsolaris.

We were acquaintances in a world of pals: women, everyone who was not from the nucleus of the bertsolaritza world, the children of immigrants, city folks. Whether it is a coincidence or not (and there are some exceptions), most of us who have moved forward in the world of bertsolaritza are the ones who have drunk the least from the goblet of tradition. Or maybe the fact that we had also drunk the most from other practices and traditions has had something to do with it. Many elements were contributing to the changes in the ecosystem of bertsolaritza. And the new, young generations not only facilitated its survival, but they also transformed the bertsolaritza world and turned it into a more interesting and motivating place to live.

New sap flowed and the bark of the tree that was bertsolaritza cracked.

A "Forced" Debut

For that young generation, neither transmission nor debuts happened in a "natural" way. They pushed us onto the stage before we were truly capable of participating in bertso slams. They were forced debuts, or sped up debuts at the very least. There was an urgency to it, probably, because of the cultural and linguistic situation. They needed young people, to renew the practice, to attract new audiences, to create points of reference in areas in which bertsolaritza was losing its grip. The desire for survival forced us to face the square, the stage, again.

> The phone rang. "I'm calling from Hondarribia," said a woman's voice, "to invite you to take part in a bertso slam: Andoni Egaña, Anjel Mari Peñagarikano, Kristina Mardaras, and you." At that point I was not really ready for a bertso slam. Improvising an eighteen-syllable *zortziko handia* in front of an audience and crossing the desert on foot seemed equally impossible to me. "No, no, no," I told her, "there's no way I can improvise bertsos against those masters." I still remember her reply: "look you: grab the bull by the horns—yeah?" I was speechless. Mute. So much so that she took my silence for acquiescence and because of that I had my second and true debut in Hondarribia.

> Grab the bull by the horns.
> They threw us into the bullring all right.

Women's Sessions

That session in Hondarribia took place on March 8, 1991. The women's organization Emeki organized a session for two men and two women. Back then, suggesting a bertso slam with such a pairing was unthinkable. It was forced. Krsitina did not really sing much. I was not ready to improvise bertsos against those two bertsolaris. But forcing things is not always bad, and the results are proof of that.

I was very fearful of and resistant to that enforcement.

They invited us "bertsolari girls" to many sessions as if we were a novelty act. The tone was very much "look at what we have here, a (bearded) woman!"

I felt that the push to perform and paternalistic attitudes were hard to separate, because, often, they did not really trust our ability to perform at a certain level. Some would hint that they could let us know the themes in advance, for example, suggesting that they did not want us to upset the balance of the session.

They wanted to show us off but they did not believe in us.

No. We made them feel insecure.

Young people in general. Women especially.

We had no lack of bertso sessions at that time. Many would say that it was easier to get a spot in a bertso competition if you were a girl, that there was "positive discrimination." "Female bertsolaris experience the worst kind of combination of discriminations: positive when they are called to perform, and negative when we judge their performance" (Egaña 1995, 57).

Because there were quite a few of us women within the young generation who had been through bertso schools, some promoters started to organize "women's sessions" here and there, sporadically. If it was a curious thing to have one girl in a bertso slam, what must it have been like having five! "Subject: what does a girl feel when taking part in a bertso slam, standing in front of a microphone?"[6]

> The first time they called me a woman I was on a stage.
> I referred to myself as a woman
> for the first time in an improvised bertso.
> Others referred to me as a woman. I would hear the word
> woman and think it did not apply to me.
> At the age of fifteen I was still a young person who had not
> developed much, ideologically speaking.
> I was not an active militant.
> We bertsolaris of this young generation have grown up in
> front of people; we have been raised by bertsolaritza.
> The world of improvised-singing put the questions to us
> before life itself did: about identity, ethics, love, and sex;
> about politics and conflict; about being a woman, equality,
> and feminism.

> I did not like the female-only sessions. They provoked
> more contradictory feelings than joy. I was cornered by a
> forceful dual push: my sense of guilt and the feeling of being
> patronized. I rebelled. We did not need that "special treat-
> ment." If we were as good as the boys and had reached their
> level, I demanded that we were lumped together with them.
> Because it was not realistic to do women-only sessions. We
> were not ready for that!

> The intention of those sessions was to scream to the
> winds that we were ready, but they showed that we were not.

> And that was counterproductive.

"Neska soileko saiorikan ez	No more women-only sessions for us,
bagera gehiorako gai.	we can do much better than that.
Gizonezkoen tarta honetan	Don't treat us like we're just the filling
Krema ez dugu izan nahi."	we're a part of this man-made tart.[7]

---

6   Pello Urretabizkaia, Lazkao, July 10, 1990, BDB, Xenpelar Dokumentazio
     Zentroa, Andoain.
7   Maialen Lujanbio, Bertso eguna, 1993.

Besides, feminism had a bad reputation at the time. Even in that left-leaning and totally Basque-loving section of society we belonged to. All of us young girls, we did not think of ourselves as feminists, even though we agreed with the bases of feminism—we wanted to belong in the team, without distinctions. Besides, most in our generation believed that we had overcome a lot of the issues feminism had fought for.

What is more, it was a difficult time politically. There was an armed conflict, a lot of tension in our society, and very intense "positioning" among us. Society was very much split in half. There was no room for nuance: everything was labeled, everything implied a positioning on one side, everything contained meaning (including feminism).

Power looked on folk culture with disdain, because it was not at its service, because it was critical, among other things. The opposition, on the other hand, tried to take ownership of everything that was in its interest.

It was not easy to keep to your path and your voice. Not so much to keep them equidistant, but rather, to keep them independent.

I tried to avoid the "women's sessions."

Was it my own sense of shame?
An internalized patriarchal way of thinking?

In my view at the time,
those sessions were counterproductive.

Time would show that forcing things is not always necessarily bad.

But, in such circumstances, back then, what was the right thing to do?

Stretch out the standard measures, get overall recognition for being better than average, and once they are listening, then try to break the mold, from within? (That would be the strategy). Or, adopting a tougher attitude, explode the mold, crush it to smithereens and start building a new, fairer one? (In the bertso world of the 1990s, this was impossible. If they did not "accept" you, if they did not listen to you, if you had no legitimacy with the audience, there was no way to break the mold).

This was going to be a very long, step-by-step kind of journey. It still is.

Heidi and Grandpa

Listening to young fifteen- and sixteen-year-old girls, in a traditional setting, attacking grown up, established male bertsolaris, besides being the only available way of gaining recognition, left a profound impact.

And when playing the parts of husband and wife, mother and son, or heterosexual couples, this added exceptional realism to the subjects. It was the first time women were singing women's parts in their own voices. "Tonight is Mañukorta and Maialen's wedding night" was the prototype for many subjects posed.

Older bertso colleagues took it upon themselves to protect and welcome us. So much so that the situation took on a paternalistic tint, because of the age difference, and because we were girls. They infantilized us. We had more of a relationship of equals with the young guys in our bertsolaritza group. There was more familiarity and mutual respect there.

"A smart young girl talks back to a grown man" soon became a too-easy, too-predictable trope. The theme prompters, likewise, were too obvious in nudging us in that direction. We were starting to get tired. If you were someone who wanted to say and be something else, the path was too narrow.

Even the initial thrill of the big applause began to fade with time. It was a double-edged sword, that kind of quick success; a dead end.

It was exhausting to always be faced by the same roles,
the same tone. I was more than that.
But which way to go? How do you reinvent yourself?
If private crises are hard,

crises in front of an audience are worse.
Besides, what was I doing? If "bertsolaritza was like that,"
if I was the last to arrive, and if it was me who felt
uncomfortable and like I did not fit in,
maybe I was in the wrong place.
Maybe I was ruining everything.
It had always been like that. Years of tradition.

It was then an eddy emerging from the encounter between two
currents: the hardened inertia of tradition and the new flow of a
young new generation.

Without a learned ideology, without a defined feminist
development, with hardly any allies, just naturally.
I was awakening and the thoughts came with it.

Like a Butterfly

The adolescent starts to grow and occupy more space and mature
and transform. By the time an adolescent is a young person, they
are also something else. Many other things.

It was time to crack the cocoon.

It was not easy. To start grabbing hold of subjects from
different places; to take those designed for an easy joke and
make them serious; to avoid the themes intended to take an
easy dig at men. At the beginning people did not understand.
For a while, I would receive hollow, scattered applause.
In the eyes of the audience,
I was wasting opportunities that were put to me on a plate.
But little by little they understood:
that I was not wasting opportunities,
but seeking new opportunities instead.
It was hard to sacrifice the applause,
but in the long run it bore fruit.

In cracking the cocoon open something different started
to emerge from the inside: more colorful and indecipherable,
more delicate and complex.

From Practice to Theory

It was the first decade of the 2000s. We had a long-enough trajectory of bertso-singing in town squares that we could start looking back. The brambles along the way had wounded us, even though we had not noticed yet. Thankfully. The thick skin of obliviousness helped us and we went on and on, moving forward. Afterward, when we looked back, we were able to identify the reasons for our wounds.

Obliviousness has its limits. The accumulation of tiny punches brought bruises to the surface in the end. We began to understand the road we had walked. The old injuries started to itch and new wounds hurt.

Starting to share our emotions with other girls from the bertso world and bertso schools was key. We understood each other immediately. It was a shared experience: spoken around plates of bean stew, years of shared experiences were brought together in a conference in Orereta in 2007 entitled "Women in bertsolaritza."

It was there that I put forward a report on the situation that reflected the experiences of many:[8]

In Bertso Schools:

- Because of their education, girls are not trained to occupy space when they play, for example, or to be the center and speak in public.

- Boys have a degree of social recognition that comes as a given, and beyond that they can do what they will (that is why boys are more daring in general; because they never doubt themselves). Girls, on the other hand, come with a given degree of doubt and then they do what they will; and they will have to do it three times better, because in fact their starting point is doubt, or a minus quantity.

- Girls from bertso schools are huge perfectionists. Perfectionists to a destructive degree. Why? Because the only way to justify being in a place where "we don't belong" is to do

---

8   Maialen Lujanbio, "Emakumea bertsolaritzan," Orereta, May 11, 2007, BDB, Xenpelar Dokumentazio Zentroa, Andoain.

the thing you are not supposed to be doing really, really well. Indisputably well.

- If bertso school just demanded writing, girls would be happy.

Adolescence:

- It is always difficult to keep up bertso-singing in this period (especially for girls). Many stop singing at this age: the most difficult aspects to overcome at that time are socialization and performing to an audience.

- There is little self-confidence in the case of girls generally: they do not believe that what they have to say matters. That the issues that are important to them are socially important. Or that they can say anything about issues that are socially important.

Facing Audiences

- Was there ever a country that attentively waited to hear what one or two girls had to say or sing? Has anyone ever listened to girls? Have they ever looked at them, allowed them to be center-stage?

- Why do we identify and suffer along with the girl who is singing? Why don't we let her be whoever she is. This is not about you. It is her turn. Detach yourself. That lone woman feels she has to represent everyone, and while we listen we feel she is representing us. It is too much responsibility. It leaves no room for failure.

- People suffer more listening to girls. Girls generate insecurity in audiences.

These were feelings that were hard to define and defend,
even though we all recognized them:
To feel taken for granted in sessions and in meetings;
to feel that words weigh differently depending on whether
they come from the mouths of men or women;
that there was no space for us to speak in those groups of
pals; that our jokes were not funny.

Underlining all those sensations was a shared experience:
**Being a woman (in command of the word) in a world
(that listens only to the voices) of men.**

Art and Ideology

To think as you live or to live as you think. We continued moving along through our experiences in town squares. Becoming increasingly aware of reality's uneven foundations.

We women always played the same roles, always archetypal, one-dimensional characters: girlfriend, mother, teacher. Men's characters were much more varied and nuanced. We started denouncing the fact that we were stuck performing "the girl in the movie" kind of roles, that we wanted to portray other kinds of women.

That sense of representing women *conditioned creativity* too: you continuously had to choose what came first: ideological content? Artistic content? When you hear "you are a farmer," "you are a soccer player," or "you are retired," and you know that the audience has automatically pictured a male, you feel the responsibility to create other possible realities in the minds of people.

Or when there was some sexist trope in the subjects we were challenged to sing too, the only woman in the session would feel "if I don't say something no one will." Men could denounce it just as well, but there was little chance that they would.

And how to denounce it in words and find the words to denounce it. In other words, how to bertso-sing a critique of it, in a way that was artistic and effective.

> *Woman, woman, woman.* I was quite tired by then, with the questions, with the responsibility, with the continuous mention of it, always the same issues.
> But it hurt me, and the things that hurt you also fuel you.

> I (and we, the women in the bertso world) were tired and, at the same time, we realized that many around us had never contemplated the issue, not even for a second.

Diffusing the Difficulties

Thanks to all the "dirty" and often silent work we had done singing in town squares, the increased presence of girls, the fact that we started talking among ourselves and shared and theorized about our sensations, and thanks to the change in mentality from the younger generations, the particular complications we had at the start began to disappear. Concern and awareness began to spread, among audiences, among the Bertso Association, among the theme prompters, and among bertsolaris themselves.

We had overcome the first few brambles, the most obvious ones. Our difficulties were beginning to diffuse. Even those of us who had been walking inside a cloud we could not see were beginning to have a clearer view of things.

When something gets diffused though, it does not disappear, it becomes harder to see and to understand, it becomes blurrier.

Bertso Day: Women's Sessions Again?

Storms were gathering among the women. Signs of thoughts, of complicity, of worries, of wanting to change, of critical ideas. You could feel it in the air, even though many did not understand where things were headed.

In 2008, with the intention of giving shape to this feeling in the air, a meeting was called by the Bertsolari Association, to propose that the next Bertso Day should have *gender* as its subject, and women should have their own session.

> Some people were in favor. Not I. For me, that was the "women's sessions" all over again; and again, I was afraid that "we shall shout that we are capable of doing this and will not be able to show that we are capable of doing it."

Rather than in 2008, in 2014 we did celebrate a Bertso Day around the subject of gender, under the title of "Surfacing," and with a group of singers composed solely of women.

It was slightly weak, artistically speaking.
But just as weak as many Bertso Days have been over the
years. Yet since this one was for women and we had to
"show" we could do it—to overcome that mistrust that
came as a given—and since it was about me and about us,
it was personally very painful.

That Bertso Day dedicated to gender left us with one hell of a
hangover. It shook us inside and out. It showed us where each one
of us stood: the bertsolaris, the fans, the supporters, and the critics.
It was not a waste of time!

Because it is not always bad to force things. According to Virginie Despentes, "[In politics] I'm not super fond of quotas, but in
practice you realize that until the time arrives when we are all truly
mixed up, all genders and races, there are always going to be deficiencies. You may have ten very sophisticated men, feminist men
and all, but in the end that won't give the same results as if you had
five guys and five girls."[9]

Work in Progress

We each evolved in our own way. But it was undeniable that in a few
short years things had changed a lot. Have changed a lot.

There are more girls singing in public, and we are increasingly
"different" among ourselves. The bertso level is getting better and
better and the variety of discourse is growing and getting stronger.

For that reason, we have different needs than before.
Each of the female singers has different needs: young women mention that they feel that they want to and need to sing
among women, because this empowers them and helps them
deal with and develop other aspects of song. On the other
hand, for those who have etched their own path and fought
to have the same recognition and the same referentiality,
that designation of "woman," that being called to sing be-

---

9   Virginie Despentes, *Otra vuelta de Tuerka*, Público TV, *Diario Público*, March
     23, 2018. At https://www.youtube.com/watch?v=3w3mrxjAV-g.

cause you are a "woman," that being classified as "woman,"
can feel diminishing and unfair.

And now, we will need opportunities to fit the space and
the moment each one of us inhabits.

Aesthetics that would not have been admitted in the previous
context are beginning to appear on stage; new clothes, voices, make-
up, body-types. For the first time, discourses that would never have
been understood or accepted in the early days are being heard in
improvised songs:

"...nire amona baita	"I can see now, looking back,
gozoa, epela	the sweetness of my grandma,
ta uste dut bera ere	her warmth, her every gesture,
lesbiana dela"	like me, she was a lesbian."
"...asko maite zaitut ta	"I love you and you know it,
gora "Bollivia."	yes oh yes to "Dykeland."[10]

The previously habitual "I didn't mean to say that she's got balls to
spare / I meant that those with balls would happily go there" and the
like are unthinkable now. Or, at least, they will not go unanswered.

And that is something too.

The text and the context have changed. The range has wid-
ened: from the realm of gastronomic societies and Basque sports,
to feminist bertso dinners; and in between those extremes, movie
theaters, youth-occupied spaces, bars, and festivals.

**New spaces have been claimed without losing the old ones.
There are all kinds of bertsolaris, ready to sing everything.**

The creative conditions are great now!
The range of subjects is much richer and more interesting.
New, in many cases. There is a whole world of terminologies
and humor to explore.

---

10   Miren Amuriza and Nerea Ibarzabal, Bizkaian Championship Final, December
17, 2016, BDB, Xenpelar Dokumentazio Zentroa, Andoain. At http://bdb.
bertsozale.eus/web/bertsoa/view/14455c.

Women's feelings of needing to "represent" are shared
around now. "If I don't say it, someone else will."
I can play, just play. Relax. As a creator, there is much more
room to develop new registers *too*.

To be rude (too), to be ugly (too), to be incorrect (too).
To put creativity before everything else, above pure ideology.
We can breathe.

**The female bertsolari has forced her entire environment to
shift. New sap is causing the tree's bark to crack.**

Complicity or the Abyss

And of course, shifts cause fear and resistance.

When I started to delve deeper into the issue of gender, I felt
an abyss had opened up between me and the men I had the greatest
complicity with. Men I had sung together with for years, men I had
known since we were very young—it was like we knew absolutely
nothing about one another.

As someone told me after the conference in Orereta: "You've
gone through all that? When did all that happen?"

We are in the same place, but we arrived there by different roads.

The things that I have experienced as a woman, by vir-
tue of being a female, I have seldom shared with my male
colleagues; my own cowardice might be to blame; perhaps
because I did not want to differentiate myself from them,
I wanted to remain on their same level, after all the work I
had put in to be a part of the team. And also, because I did
not feel much of an interest or a disposition to listen, com-
ing from them; or because I could sniff their fear and their
discomfort; or because I did not sense any willingness to
understand from them; or because I did not coincide 100
percent with the younger female singers' initial reading of
things; there must be a reason why our generation has not
talked about these subjects in depth.

We accelerated the changes and the complications in everything related to gender. Down the years, many people had worked on this subject—within themselves and publicly in bertso sessions. And now, bertsolaritza cannot escape those questions anymore.

Men, in the best cases, agree in theory, but find it hard to really *see* things. Women, on the other hand, are experientially *there*. Because they live it, because they have worked on it ideologically—that is why they *see* it all. They see the gender imbalance in everything.

Men, these days, in some contexts, are the acquaintances in the circles of pals. They are the *other*. They are uncomfortable. This is not something to be happy about, but it is a curious thing: they now sometimes inhabit the space we used to always live in. The earth is stirring under our feet, and this causes fear and a loss of direction.

> For all of us. For me as well. I am learning a way to create and sing bertsos I don't quite command it yet.
> We learned to play soccer and now the game is changing.

> Discomfort is the best place to start.

Regardless of the fear, the group of humans that live and breathe bertsolaritza and the Bertsolaritza Association itself combine to make an abundant, generous ground that is always willing to work through subjects like these. Even before now, it was our open disposition that brought us this far.

Now

With the help of contemporary, current feminist discourse, the artistic and theoretical work carried out in the bertso world and the general newfound awareness among audiences, the game is changing in the public spaces in which we sing our bertsos.

The subjects set for us are changing; they are better suited to the current realities and to addressing present conflicts; the subjects themselves, and the treatment of the subjects. The form of our performances, the bodily attitudes and the voices too, are changing. The very heart of the bertsos themselves is changing: the humor code, the references, the ideas, the singing tones; what discourse is acceptable, what is legitimate, what subjects are interesting, what subjects are for everyone, how should certain topics be dealt with, what is politically correct and what is not; a lot of content is in the process of transformation, some of it in doubt.

The rising tide of empowerment has its risks too:
Some of the characteristics of bertsolaritza are essential:
the voice, the song, the ability to communicate,
doing it in the presence of an audience.
What is negotiable, always, is how this is done, but we
should never lose sight of these essential aspects.

We should revise the form of bertsolaritza, but we must always be careful to maintain the presential aspect, the voice, the modes of singing. For theory to go ahead of prac-tice. In our case, they asked us the questions before we had experience and, now, the new generations know the answers before they have any experience. Lucky them!

But this always having a ready-made political reading of things can lead to a hollow attitude of perpetual complaint.
It can lead to lowering what we demand of ourselves.
Being able to read the imbalance in things should not be a comfortable hiding place from which we don't even bother to try.

We have increased our critical capabilities. Now it is time to raise our level of creativity to the same, or an even higher, level. To use ideology artistically. Those young people who have so much that is so good to say, they should learn to say it in sung bertsos, in ways that can become influential.

Put aside victimhood,
without stopping denouncing things.
Put aside complaining,
without giving up on anger.

Munduko euskal hiztune (bis)	Now my people my Basque pack (x2)
geroa dena beltzune...	I know the future is bleak…
Bada garaia eranzteko	but it's time to say that's it
lepoko zama astune,	that weight they put on your rack
bestek erantsi dotzune...	best thing is to give it back
zeuk kendu beharko dozune!	I swear it's a lot of whack![11]

And what applies to the Basque pack, also applies to women.

We have to keep working from within the structure while we simultaneously try to change the structure.

To Sum Up

Bertsolaritza has changed a lot in a few short years. The work that started in bertso school has borne fruit. Bertsolaritza has been renewed, it has multiplied, and been rejuvenated.

Daring to risk things and an open-minded attitude are the reasons why bertsolaritza is in full health today.

It is to be expected that when the time comes to fully incorporate women's perspectives, this art form will continue to play a generous, brave hand. It is, in fact, doing just that, slowly.

The chain has not broken and the older bertsolaris are alert to the contributions of the younger generations. The act of singing bertsos is a neverending process of adaptation.

Women bertsolaris are an essential part of today's movement. More and more women who have nothing in common are a part of it. This aspect brings new artistic content into the form and will continue doing so. We will hear voices we have not heard yet, types of women we have not even imagined yet.

We cannot name a generation the *women's* generation. Because it has protagonists of different ages. It is more like a powerful influx

---

11   Maialen Lujambio, "Baltza nazela diñeure," bertso performance, Bilbo, December 29, 2016.

of perspectives that were missing in the world of bertsolaritza. An alternative interpretation of the form and an artistic and ideological proposal adapted to it.

The processes of reflection, consciousness, and creativity are increasingly significant and transgressive. Women are rethinking things collectively, gaining awareness, and pouring feminist ideology into their bertsos.

Male bertsolaris, bertso schools, audiences in general, theme prompters, judges, and members of the Bertsolaritza Association have started to develop a gender perspective.

Over and over again, new sap causes the tree's bark to crack.

The earth is stirring.

It will be as uncomfortable as it will be inspiring.

Bibliography

"Bertso eskolek 25 urte." *Argia*, February 24, 2018.

Egaña, Andoni. "Inkesta. Hiru galdera bertsolariei." *Bertsolari* (Spring 1995): 57.

Esteban, Mari Luz. *Antropología del cuerpo. Género, itinerarios corporales, identidad y cambio.* Barcelona: Ediciones Bellaterra, 2004.

Garzia, Joxerra, Jon Sarasua, and Andoni Egaña. *The Art of Bertsolaritza: Improvised Basque Verse Singing.* Donostia: Bertsozale Elkartea, 2001.

CHAPTER 4

Contemporary Women Bertsolari
The Tale of a Possible
Empowerment Process[1]

Miren Artetxe Sarasola

> "Feminism has nourished us, it has opened
> doors, windows, for us; we have seen things that
> we did not used to see, but what we want is to sing and have
> a good time, basically."

> Ainhoa Agirreazaldegi Rekondo[2]

It was not so long ago that the term "woman bertsolari" was an
oxymoron. Nowadays, however, any Basque will tell you that Ane
Labaka, Aroa Arrizubieta, Eli Pagola, Jone Uria, Nahia Sasco,

---

1   Without going into any deeper definitions, here the word "women" is
     understood in terms of "socialized as women" and "interpreted as women."
     This work was supported by the Department of Education, Linguistic Policy,
     and Culture of the Basque government (IT-881-16).
2   *Contenedor de feminismos: Docu-acción para el contenedor de feminismos. Mujeres
     bertsolaris* (2014), documentary film, at https://www.youtube.com/
     watch?v=XRhd4wi8T5E.

Nerea Ibarzabal, and countless others are bertsolaris, without any conceptual problem.

Undeniably, though, the hegemonic bertsolari is still a man and to a great extent the bertsolaritza system has made and continues to make that hegemonic bertsolari (Larrañaga 1994; Hernández 2006). Indeed, bertsolaritza is not a social and cultural practice that develops in an isolated way outside of society, and therefore the gender system that traverses society from top to bottom also traverses bertsolaritza.

Yet on the way to opening up a concept from the oxymoron of bodies, bertsolaritza itself has embraced many changes from a gender perspective. And women in the bertso world have developed these changes, in both calculated as well as intuitive ways, individually and collectively.

In this chapter, I propose interpreting some of the milestones in the transformation process of women bertsolaris, mostly since about the turn of the millennium. I do not just want to explain what changes have taken place and where we are right now; I would also like to examine several key events, moments, and places in getting here. Clearly, wider social changes have also influenced the development of bertsolaritza in recent years, and in this regard my focus of inquiry will be several moments and places of change through initiatives promoted by people in the bertso world. And if personal trajectories have also had an influence in the bertso world itself, in both bertsogintza and in the structure of the bertsolaritza system, then in this chapter I will pay attention—to some extent at least—to initiatives that have been developed collectively.[3]

---

3   For example, in this chapter I will not examine the influence that Maialen Lujanbio's personal trajectory (in winning the Basque national championship in 2009 and 2017) has had directly in bertsogintza and the bertsolaritza system as well as throughout the individual and collective trajectories of women bertsolaris, even though it has been crucial in this process. The truth is that focusing on collective elements responds to a pragmatic incentive: because I myself am a member of the bertso movement and a feminist, I would like this text to represent the reflections of women bertsolaris, in its own humble way, looking toward the future in order to consider the steps we may take collectively to achieve (more) equality in bertsolaritza.

In order to do so, as regards my approach, I will adopt an autoethnographic perspective;[4] and I have based my methodology on direct observation, the analysis of performances, surveys sent out to women bertsolaris,[5] and document analysis.

The Iceberg:
The Tip, Underwater, and the Current

The iceberg metaphor is a useful lens on a specific and obvious situation of everything beneath the surface. As noted, bertsolaritza has changed a lot—above all when looking from a gender perspective— in recent years. As a result of the bertso schools, the public appearance of women bertsolaris has not just been legitimized but has become normal, possessing a woman's voice has not de facto rendered us incapable of creating bertsos, in general the themes have been adapted to the potential presence of women, and one sees more and more women in bertso sessions—public as well as in contests—beyond just March 8, international women's day. Certain changes could be viewed as anecdotal if taken in isolated fashion, but one could say that together they reveal structural changes. Of course it is not the same thing, when taking about equality of opportunity, to be a woman or a man in bertsolaritza, insofar as both society and the bertsolaritza system itself impose boundaries. Yet there is an idea that I would place on the tip of the iceberg, that is, what I identify as the latest summit in all the changes that have taken place: namely, as well as women adapting to bertsolaritza, there is also a clear political demand for the bertsolaritza system itself to be more inclusive for women.

---

4   As Jone Miren Hernández (1999) and Mari Luz Esteban (2004b) have contended, the research process cannot be completely separated from one's own experience. Nor should we want it to be: I believe that starting with a critical take on my own experience can enrich other's understanding.

5   I posed four questions to several women bertsolaris, to be answered in written and open form. Fundamentally, I asked them to give a specific definition of empowerment, in order to identify the moments and places that served them as regards being empowered as bertsolaris and women, and to reflect on what was missing in those processes. Twenty-three colleagues answered those questions. My thanks to you all.

I would contend that there is, within the contemporary bertso movement itself, at least an awareness of the need to take the gender perspective into consideration, and from the basis of that awareness we are witnessing several restructuring attempts in the bertso world – not without great effort, nor without some resistance either. But, above all at the discursive level, the politically correct idea is developing—even if not among all the people involved in this world and at different levels among those people—that bertsolaritza itself is responsible, specifically, for adapting its system to women bertsolaris.

In order to bring that idea to ocean level, however, a route has been constructed, as mentioned. Besides the changes that have taken place in society thanks to academia and the feminist movement as well as at the discursive level and in practice, this change has been due specifically to the many initiatives on the part of women bertsolaris in order to meet their needs in formal and informal ways, both consciously and unconsciously, and individually as well as collectively. And I would like to highlight several defining moments in this trajectory: the contribution of the first reference points, the creation of a women bertsolari network, and bringing feminist theory and practice to bertsolaritza. Ultimately, I will argue that this trajectory has been at root an empowering process[6] and, looking toward the future, I will conclude with several reflections on the possibility of continuing with this empowerment.

The First Contemporary Reference Points[7]

---

6   I am aware of the fact that using the concept of empowerment can bring with it a certain ambiguity and the risks involved with such ambiguity (Esteban 2017). I will discuss this in more detail below. I would say, however, that I have decided to employ this concept because it has been used a lot in the bertso world since first appearing in the Basque Country in 2003, and because I understand that the polysemy of the concept in these models is being neutralized, thereby limiting the associated risks.

7   Women bertsolaris have appeared throughout the history of bertsolaritza. For instance, the first reference we have is that of a ban on women bertsolaris taking part in bertsolaritza. Women were singing in the early nineteenth-century challenges at the birth of modern bertsolaritza. Yet in the transformation from bertsolaritza being part of the landscape to being part of culture (Laborde 2005) and, at the same time, as the definition of bertsolaritza became strictly connected to improvised rather than written activity (Larrañaga 1997), so the names of women bertsolaris began to disappear from contemporary

Although I want to concentrate on the period since the turn of the millennium and especially on collective initiatives, one cannot do so without mentioning the first women points of reference in contemporary bertsolaritza.

Amaia Otsoa, Kristina Mardaras, and Arantzazu Loidi were the first women to appear during the age of contemporary bertsolaritza singing in public in the 1980s. The bertso schools were already functioning at this time, and the new generations appearing on the public stage were made up of young girls and boys. That is how, for example, Estitxu Arozena, Iratxe Ibarra, Ainhoa Agirreazaldegi, and Maialen Lujanbio (among many others) also came to public prominence in the 1990s.

One could say that women's voices and bodies were still battlefields at this time, with one of the main problems being that women bertsolaris' bodies themselves were non-hegemonic,[8] as were their voices as well. One could speculate, then, that women bertsolaris at that time were obliged, publically through their bodies and voices, to confront many prejudices and taboos, with bertsolaritza inevitably shaping their presence according to the moment and the place, even if they were not fully accepted.

That said, the subversion of those women did not just derive from those bodies appearing on stages. They also brought the conflict to a discursive level. They put words to that tension, for the first time, and in the first person. Indeed, thanks to those bodies, women could speak for the first time from the position of women's roles (as that was what most of themes associated with them demanded, because they were only allowed to speak about such roles), although not just about women; for example, they also addressed bertsolaritza.[9]

---

chronicles as well as history books. It was only at the end of the nineteenth century that people began to hear women singing once more in improvised and public spaces.

8   Basically, "because female bodies were not the site of bertsos" (Hernández 2016, 17). For more on this topic, see, moreover, Esteban (2004a) and Alberdi (2014).

9   The following, taken from the 1993 Bertsolari Day in a session involving Lujanbio, Ibarra eta Arozena, demonstrates this, especially in a bertso by Arozena: (Donostia, January 24, 1993) "Emakumeok mikrofonoan

This discursive level tension also brought about changes, adapt-ing male bertsolaris to the women's discourse; although, obviously, not straight away or completely. But without a doubt the boundaries of political correctness shifted. Clearly at the social level the times were changing; and as Karine Etxeberri (2015, 47) clearly explains, "the problem of gender equality in the bertsolaritza movement was equally one of contextualization within the women's movement."[10] And those women were front and center in forcing the generational change within bertsolaritza itself.[11]

I would underscore just how influential it could have been being a reference point during a time of progress in a practice; or perhaps put more explicitly, not being a point of reference. Estitxu Eizagirre (2005) recounts the influence of Maialen Lujanbio as just such a reference point:

> When we began doing bertsos we began by writing, and we were very hooked on writing. And we went to one school championship, and there I saw a girl singing for the first time. And I remember that, at the age of eight, I thought to myself: "Ah, of course, it's possible for a girl to sing." And my next thought was: "Well, just like in soccer, while they're kids it's ok, sure, but there aren't any professionals." A few years later I saw Maialen on televi-sion, and that's when my problems started, because I saw that it was possible for a girl to appear alongside Lizaso,

/ jaso izan dugu burla. / Gaur ere batzuk haserre daude, / ezin dute disimula. / Ni ziur nago egunen baten / erakutsiko dugula / bertsolaritzak barrabilekin / zerikusirik ez dula" (Stepping up to the microphone, / we women have been taunted. / Even today some people are mad, / they can't hide it. / I'm sure that one day / we'll show that / bertsolaritza has nothing / to do with balls).

10 Above all, by that time there had been three Feminist Encounters of the Basque Country meetings (in 1977, 1984, and 1994) and the Basque feminist movement was gaining strength (Zabala 2008; Epelde, Aranguren, and Retolaza 2015).

11 One sign of that generational change, for example, was Andoni Egaña's parting bertso (the *agurra*) at the 1997 National Championship: (Donostia, December 14, 1997) "Ez da bakarrik Belodromoko / jendetza honen disdira / bertsolaritza aurrera doa / emakumeen harira / 82ko Txapelketari / jarri gaitezen begira / orduan gaitzat hartzen genitun / ta orain eurak gai dira" (This glow isn't just / down to the crowds here in the velodrome, / bertsolaritza is forging ahead / following the direction of women. / Just take a look at / the 82 championship. / Then we looked at them badly, / and now they're more than capable).

and from then on it was more difficult to carry on writing bertsos alone in my favorite notebook; I had to take the next step and sing and improvise in front of people, and that was a problem for me.

It is not enough, however, just to be a point of reference in a sys-tem in which male bertsolaris are hegemonic if women bertsolaris do not overcome the obstacles in successive generations. One may think it somewhat naïve to say that if there is someone to blaze a trail in the first place, for those that come later there are less hurdles. Carmen Larrañaga expresses this idea very well, in fact, in a work published the same year Egaña sang the aforementioned bertso. For her, the existence of several reference points in itself does not necessarily make it easier for those that come later to carry on in the same direction:

> And it is argued that after her [Kristina Mardaras], navigat-ing the trail of bertsolaritza was much easier for the few women improvisers that followed. This is only partially true. History teaches us that before Mardaras there were other bertsolaris with sufficient skill to win even public contests, without their participation encouraging any gender balance (men and women) in the exercise of bertsolaritza (Larrañaga 1997, 60).

In order to call into question the very system of bertsolaritza itself, and to take into account a gendered perspective of the people that socialized bertsolaritza, it is not enough for some women to carve out a new direction, even though without that it is impossible to progress either. There are several other key factors when it comes to changing course.

The First Thread in the Network

Nowadays, unlike fifty years ago, the first step for a young person wanting to get into bertsolaritza, if they do not do so at home in the family, is, typically and most often, in bertso school. There one meets weekly—for a couple of hours or so—with one's classmates in order to study how to create improvised bertsos.[12] Later, they may or may not end up performing in public. Yet bertso school is essentially a place in which, whatever the age, to do group work on improvisation. The group is the foundation of the bertso school. The relationships among group members will define the atmosphere of the bertso school, and bertso school students will be fellow travelers when it comes to socializing in the wider bertso world; to go an listen to others' or their fellow bertso school students' sessions; to get to know people from other bertso schools; to speak about bertsolaritza or the bertso world; in other words, to socialize with people that share the same fondness for bertsolaritza.

The truth is that in children's bertso schools it is customary for there to be as many girls as boys in the group, but as they get older, there are still more boys than girls. The imbalance most often takes place in the jump from writing to improvisation and from closed groups to the public space: many girls leave bertso school (Latasa 2010). Many factors may influence this phenomenon—those at the social level, and almost certainly in interaction those that consciously correspond to bertsogintza and the bertso world—and they deserve more profound examination, but the issue is that many girls end up being the only girl in bertso school from a certain age onward.

Consequently, girl bertsolaris have had limited options when it comes to singing, talking, or just being with other girl bertsolaris. When that used to happen, moreover, it was often in the context of a competition, whether a school championship or a young persons' contest. When I was younger, there was no municipal space or any special option for bertsolaritza-related free-time activity for young people of our age. It was not at all typical to see more than one girl signing in a bertso session—with the exception of those on March 8—and there were still many sessions without any girls at all.

That is why the women bertsolaris' meetings held in 2003 marked such a watershed moment. Fifteen of us, ranging in age from twenty to thirty, met together. And in many cases, we did not know each

---

12 It is customary, at the outset, in children's bertso schools to first develop their written skills, and later take the step toward improvised activities. In young adult's bertso schools, improvised skills mostly form the chief activity.

other. In one participant's word: "We followed our intuition in spending the weekend in Askizu; we knew there was something in that topic, but we were not sure what . . . Of course, drawing up a list of girls in the bertso world, and getting to know one another as well because speaking by email with people we did not know was "artificial," or "organized" rather than organic. Yes, spending that weekend there was all about bertsos and women" (Eizagirre 2004, 2). That weekend, we shared our experiences as women bertsolaris; without any organized topics; where we felt the boundaries lay; whether we were settled or unsettled.

Estitxu Eizagirre lists some of the concerns that were raised in a chronicle of that encounter:

> Why do they call us, in order to fulfill a gender quota or because we are who we are? Is it bad to call us because we are girls? Who does the theme prompter think about when setting the themes? Why do I always play the woman's role? Why is it so difficult for bertso school girls to perform in public? The embarrassment, fear, stage fright they feel . . . what influences this? Do I have my own bertso style or do I imitate [the male bertsolari]? Why must I listen to the idea circling around me that the women's issue has been resolved? If society is sexist, is it possible for bertsolaritza to be immune to this? Do we appear in public as we would like to? Some of us have given up along the way . . . why? (Eizagirre 2004, 1–2).

I also recall two things that impacted me a lot: first, realizing, surprisingly (for me at the time), that the experiences, questions, and concerns of the other women resembled my own experiences, questions, and concerns. I remember how each problem and struggle resonated with me.

That confirmation brought with it a second realization: there was a structure that created similar experiences for me and the other women. I recall a feeling of liberation—to some extent—taking part on an uneven playing field. It was not me. It was the structure. And we did not occupy the best place in that structure – acknowledging that is easier than someone feeling an intrinsic inability or incapacity.

My analysis was, then, as clumsy as it was clear: in our understanding, what men did was what was done to be a bertsolari; yet we could not do everything that men did. Not because we were incapable, but because it was not legitimate for us to do so. It did not work. The boundaries of humor and speech hemmed us in too much.[13] The gaze of other bertsolaris and the public did not seek out our talent. We did very well, *for girls*.[14] The rules of the game were not the same for everyone and any achievement was more difficult for us; indeed, any achievement at all was a pleasure.

It may seem surprising, when it had been ten years since the session by Arozena, Ibarra, and Lujanbio at that Bertsolari Day, and at a time when bertsolaritza was a practice almost entirely still run by men, that for many of us in 2003 the gendered structure of bertsolaritza was not evident. Yet this paradox is applicable, unfortunately, to all other kinds of social and cultural practices, and ours was no exception. Moreover, at that time, those of us who met in Alkizu were not pioneering women bertsolaris, and that made our experiences seem milder. We were not starting from scratch. We did not have to adapt so much, never in fact, to being the first women to sing in a specific public setting or to any rules necessarily being changed to allow us to enter. Since we had begun to sing, it had not been politically correct to say that a woman could not be a bertsolari. By that time, it was a time of more clearly defined boundaries.[15]

---

13   Iratxe Ibarra highlighted the asymmetrical rules of the game when she sang in that well-known Bertsolari Day with Arozena and Lujanbio: "Erabiltzen den hizkerak ere / badu nahiko zerikusi / guk neskok kontu horretan behintzat / ez baitugu hola bizi / nahiz ta gizonek kristonak esan / beren grazi eta guzi / *de puta madre* geratzen zaie / ta guri berriz itsusi" (The form of speech used too / has a lot do with it / because in that regard we girls at least / have not experienced that / even though men are great at expressing / their humor and everything / it looks *fucking great* on them / yet ugly on us).

14   "For people to recognize that a girl is good at doing bertsos, she has to be good on three occasions. It is not enough to be good once. The first year, quite good, 'you're pretty good for a girl'. Later, after a few more years, 'well, the best out of all the girls'. And then, perhaps, you may be told that you're a good bertsolari. Thus, you have to be good three times, for people to say 'she creates bertsos', now it's not good or bad, but the fact that she creates bertsos" (Lujanbio 2007).

15   In 1999, when Arozena herself asked her father (and also a bertsolari) Manolo Arozena about the bertsos she sang at the 1993 session, at a session in Goizueta, Navarre, she mentioned the invisible structures: (Goizueta, August 17, 1999) "Oinarri txarrak baldin baditu / aldatzen dira ohiturak; /

Jone Miren Hernández, meanwhile, highlights the fact that, in what was at that point an influential book about contemporary bertsolaritza, Joxerra Garzia, Jon Sarasua, and Andoni Egaña (2001, 28) assert that, "the presence of women bertsolaris has long ceased to be a significant anecdote." The hegemonic discourse of the bertso world did not explicitly marginalize us. However, the belief that we had reached a supposedly normal situation made it more difficult, specifically, to see, identify, and designate the obstacles.

Feminist Theories in Bertsolaritza, and Bertsolaritza in Feminism

Any analysis of the (re)incorporation of women into new spaces requires going beyond the importance of the number of women that participate currently, to analyzing the mechanisms of segregation, of inequality, that are more much more subtle and for that reason more difficult to detect. The originate in universes in which inequality has impregnated forms of being, of dressing, of behaving, of gesticulating, of competing, of dialectic resolution, of getting emotional. On this basis, the feminist anthropological gaze can expose the deep structures that function in the expressions, language, symbols, [and] imaginary, and only from that analysis is it possible to discover the substrates of differences that are turned into inequalities, in this case, into the access to equality for spaces of power and privilege (Del Valle 2012, 12).

---

bidetxiorrik ez izan arren / bidea egin du urak. / Haseran garbi izan genitun / eredu eta helmugak, / arriskutsuen bihurtu dira / ikusten ez diren mugak" (If one has bad foundations / the customs change; / even though there is no way / water carves out a way. / We had a clear idea at first / about the model and the objectives, / the unseen boundaries / became dangerous). Likewise, Arantzazu Loidi herself, in a 1995 interview for a monograph on women bertsolaris titled "Emakumeak Plazara" by the journal *Bertsolari*, was asked "Between the time you were singing and now does the state of bertsolaritza have the same characteristics?" She replied: "I think it is getting better, I think some obstacles have been overcome. Those of us who initially emerged had to wear a kind of veil. Now things are done in a clearer way. There is no kind of wall that needs breaking down in order to sing in public. In that sense it is more advanced. But some things, which are very subtle, and because of that, still persist" (Loidi 1995, 40).

Since the Askizu meeting, the topic of gender has been front and center in bertsolaritza as well. Examples of that, for instance, include the monographic episode about women on the bertsolaritza television show *Hitzetik Hortzera* in 2005, the articles published by several women bertsolaris on different blogs, the *Emetik Bertso Kabareta* (Female bertso cabaret) show created by Onintza Enbeita, Iratxe Ibarra, and Oihane Perea in 2006, Maialen Lujanbio's 2007 lecture "Bertsolaritza emakumearen ikuspuntutik: bertsolaritza eta emakumea" (Bertsolaritza from a woman's perspective: Bertsolaritza and women) (Lujanbio 2007), the roundtable discussion titled "And Gender" organized by the journal *Argia* in 2008 (Eizagirre 2008), and the creation of the Gender Group.[16] As well as all these developments, by that time feminist anthropology had already started to address what was happening in bertsolaritza[17] and the feminist movements continued to go from strength to strength in the Basque Country (Zabala 2008; Epelde, Aranguren, and Retolaza 2015).

However, still at that time within the bertso world the terms "bertsolari(tza)" and "feminist" were not syntagmatic, at least not outside the academic world. In this regard, Uxue Alberdi and Ainhoa Agirreazaldegi were pioneers. Using the tools of feminism and more specifically feminist anthropology, incorporating an interpretation of the influence that the gender system has typically had in society, interpreting from feminist discourse topics that had at that time emerged once more, and looking at bertsolaritza from a feminist perspective, these two bertsolaris argued for new explanations in the analysis. They gave a talk, "Bertsolaritza: A Feminist Gaze," over forty times between 2010 and 2015. One could say they took an academic argument and popularized it.

---

16   In 2008, following a process of reflection, the first working structure purposely in favor of equality was created within the most important reference point association in the bertso world: the Association of Friends of Bertsolaritza Gender Group (Erkiaga 2008).

17   Above all we are indebted to Jone Miren Hernández for this. She was the first person to examine how the gender system runs through bertsolaritza (Hernández 2006). Likewise, Mari Luz Esteban's focus on women bertsolaris' bodies was also influential (Esteban 2004a). Thereafter, among other examples, came Leire Ibarguren's master's thesis on how women use humor on stage (Ibarguren 2009).

In that talk, meanwhile, they underscored the strategic nature of a feminist consciousness in order to construct a non-marginalizing bertsolaritza. Furthermore, they understood the changes that a feminist consciousness would bring to bertsolaritza as a contribution to making it richer because it would bring about a non-marginalizing idea. And finally, looking ahead, they argued for a closer relationship between the feminist movement and people in the bertso world, in both directions. Feminism offered the tools for bertsolaritza to become more equal, and bertsolaritza also had something to offer on the way to a more equal society. For the first time, we were women, bertsolaris, and feminists. Or at least we could be.

That formulated discourse created a truly possible hypothetical scenario to build a relationship between the feminist movements and bertsolaritza. Thus, for example, it led those of us who did not have a direct relationship with the feminist movement to look toward feminism.[18] And as well as that, comparing the experience of women in bertsolaritza with that of women in other fields, the experience gained from other fields facilitated that bridge-building work among people in academia, the feminist movement, and the bertso world.

Feminist Practices in Bertsolaritza: *It is No Coincidence* and the *Empowering Bertso School*

That is how, since then, several practices have emerged within bertsolaritza that would be difficult to justify without feminist discourse. For example, creating non-mixed fields, outside of those meetings, in public activities and stage skills.

The context was no longer the same as in 2003. Yet the topic of gender was more important than ever in the bertso world, thanks to

---

18 "For me, personally, if feminism is something new, it has been thanks to women bertsolaris. That has always been a nearby source," according to the bertsolari Nerea Ibarzabal in an interview at the 2017 National Bertsolaritza Championship (Ibargutxi 2017).

that talk.[19] And as regards the public space, a number of transforma-
tive initiatives were created: non-mixed sessions—or at least those
clearly made up mostly of women—such as, chiefly, the performance
titled *Ez Da Kasualitatea* (It is no coincidence).[20] That same title had
been given to a 2009 musical show, made up entirely of women, in
Mutriku, Gipuzkoa; and from that time on the format was repeated
on several other occasions, and especially from 2013 onward, going
from strength to strength. In those sessions, women sing alongside
women, and joining together in song we have realized the extent of
the influence that women bertsolaris have when they sing together.
One could cite several examples of this influence, but here I will
take the following into consideration: a confident atmosphere and
an awareness of the strength and value of one's voice.

On the one hand, usually there has been an especially empathetic
atmosphere among the bertso colleagues in these performances. We
have typically demonstrated such mutual understanding through
both gestures and words, both on and off stage. And that accumu-
lation of performing experience builds up a network of complicity
(Labaka 2017; Alberdi 2015). On the other hand, there are two im-
portant elements: first, in this kind of session women bertsolaris are
not concerned about feeling like or potentially feeling like a token
when they are the only woman, breaking several boundaries that
are placed on them when they feel like that. And second, because
these performances attract a largely female audience, a more shared
self-referential world—to some extent—with the public is usually
created. Thus, we bertsolaris feel freer to say and do what we would
not do in other sessions (Labaka 2017).

---

19   The Association of Friends of Bertsolaritza Gender Group began to organize
      meetings among women bertsolaris, and in 2013 we met again in Alkizu,
      transforming those encounters into annual meeting points. The 2014 Bertso
      Day was organized around gender, and in 2015 the show *Bertsolaritzaren
      Sekretuak. Isilduriko emakumeen historia* (The secrets of bertsolaritza: The silent
      history of women) premiered; that is, the subject was now public, and very
      topical.
20   The title itself demonstrates, to some extent, the nature of the performance:
      namely, that it was no coincidence that most—indeed, almost all—of the
      bertsolaris on stage were women.

Ultimately, in such sessions what we feel is an atmosphere of confidence. And that brings with it an increased confidence for anyone involved. Asked about how she feels in such performances, Alberdi answers in the following way (2015): "Especially comfortable. In normal sessions I feel like it's a competition, the need to demonstrate something . . . And in these ones I don't feel that so much. I feel like my voice has something to say, and that in itself gives me strength. Moreover, very motivated, and that motivation also encourages me to take risks."

And that issue of confidence is not insignificant. At the 2014 women bertsolaris' meeting, when we asked ourselves, by means of collective reflection, "What do I need to be good at creating bertsos?" the almost unanimous response was *confidence* (whether confidence in someone, or spaces of confidence). We realized that we were aware, naturally, that we were capable of creating bertsos; moreover, that we wanted to do so. And what we need to do that well—and what, to a large extent, we lacked—was a belief in ourselves.[21] For that, more spaces would lead us to that much needed belief in ourselves. From that deduction, specifically, another strategic space that we may define as a means of feminist practice in the bertso world emerged: the *empowering bertso school.*

In 2015 the Gender Group proposed the setting up of a bertso school especially for women bertsolaris, with the goal of *empowering* those bertsolaris who wanted to perform in public. This model is also influential when it comes to indicating the value and strength of an individual and group, and also when women bertsolaris become more aware and create networks.[22] As stated above, women bertsolaris do not have a lot of specific spaces for themselves in which to meet, and even less regular times to get together. When we do

---

21 In a study about the reasons that women bertsolaris give up bertsolaritza, Izarne Zelaia (2015) concludes that one of the main reasons they do so, at least, a "lack of confidence" (hand in hand with being too self-demanding), is clearly structural, and that the root of this is the reproduction of the gender system in education.

22 The bertsolari Oihana Iguaran (Piedra 2017) observes the following of the empowering bertso school: "A big group of women have come together, strengthened by listening to one another, we believed each one of could contribute something, without any inhibitions."

meet, it is most often at an around public performances. And the empowering bertso school—as well as a place in which to become familiar with bertso improvisation—is a space in which to share experiences and reflections. Unlike the public spaces, free of the pressure of an audience, it allows for us to reflect on our activity; to get a perspective at the end of the day: In the words of woman bertsolari Amaia Agirre, "we make our concerns known; when we are comfortable and uncomfortable in bertso sessions; sometimes it could be because of the theme, because we don't know enough about it, or when we don't know how to respond to something formulated by a bertso colleague . . . we have detected a lot of situations" (Goenaga Lizaso 2017).

There are several ideas that resonate in the statements about what I have defined as feminist practices. In each case, we reflect on the issues that emerge as regards the public space, the themes, the audience, the organizers, our bertso colleagues, and ourselves, and share those reflections. And in each case, we experiment with new environments, tones, and styles of humor in bertsos, consciously sometimes and unconsciously other times. In the words of Teresa del Valle (2012, 18), this is "a complete challenge that requires and demonstrates empowerment and creativity."

Facilitating a Move toward Equality in Bertsolaritza: Final Reflections

If bertsolaritza has been transformed in recent years as regards the gender perspective, it has to a large extent been thanks to several initiatives carried out by women bertsolaris. It has not been enough just for some women to blaze a trail when it comes to calling the bertsolaritza system into question, even though without that no progress would have been possible. There are several other key factors that have come into play on the road to change. On the one hand, creating a network led us to be aware of structure, to be able to share experiences, and to study each other's experiences. The feminist theorization that came to bertsolaritza carried out bridge-building work between the feminist movement and bertsolaritza, making the experience of women in bertsolaritza comparable to women's experience in other fields, and thereby facilitating the bringing of feminist practices outside bertsolaritza to the bertso world. We are, therefore, giving shape to new ways of understanding bertsolaritza, in public and not in public, in women's bertso sessions, and in bertso schools: "In the twentieth century, the male public model dominated. And in the twenty-first century? A prediction: bertsolaritza is heading toward a new definition, and, in this, the contribution of women will be indispensable. Bertsos are full of women's experiences, emotions, melodies, wishes, and demands, in order to be able to portray a bertsolaritza for everyone" (Hernández 2011b, 3).

This is only the beginning and there is still a long wide road ahead in order to reach equality in bertsolaritza, as Hernández explains quite clearly (2016). The gender system permeates bertsolaritza and discrimination rooted in the gender dichotomy is found at all levels of bertsolaritza (Hernández 2016). In this situation, if we want an area in which each person can benefit from bertsogintza and the bertso world, and so that if we want, our contemporary and future bertso colleagues as well, we must keep on signing (as much as we can, as well as we can, and, above all, as enjoyably as we can), keep on examining critically how the gender system pervades bertsolaritza, and breaking the balance of that system; in other words, keep on empowering.

In that sense, if, following Kate Young (2006, 4–5), we understand empowerment as a radical change in the process and structure that reproduces the subordinate position of women—and if we take it as given that we would prefer those major changes to take place in a shorter rather than longer time-frame—we could more easily understand that collective actions are essential as well as individual empowerment (ibid. 5): "women become empowered through collective reflection and decision-making. Its parameters are building a positive self image and self-confidence, developing the ability to think critically, building up group cohesion and fostering decision-making and action" (Government of India 1986, in ibid., 123).

Empowerment as a concept has become as ambiguous as it is invoked, however, in recent years (Esteban 2017), and in bertsolaritza as well. And just as we define empowerment, so we will also carry out an analysis and evaluation of the women's empowerment process. It is striking to me how, nor in the discourses of women bertsolaris that take part in collective structures do we still give much space to the collective dimension of empowerment either. It seems to me strategic, then, looking to the future, to add the collective dimension to the concept of empowerment as well as to continue to reflect on how we can and how we want to be women bertsolaris collectively.

Nowadays, numerous feminist discourses and practices create and recreate spaces in bertsolaritza and they enjoy more and more centrality in the bertso world. More and more of us define ourselves as active participants in that process. We appear in public, we are theme prompters, educators, judges, organizers, and many of us are in one way or another also involved in bertsolaritza in an academic way, studying it from a gender perspective; we write newspaper and magazine columns, we are on Twitter, and we are members of Basque, provincial, and local bertso aficionado associations. And if we understand that empowerment influences the bertsolaritza system collectively from the feminist space, we should also reflect on the relationship between feminist spaces in the bertso world and the bertso system as a whole as well as the dynamics within the collective of women bertsolaris. In that sense, I would like to ask the questions posed by Mari Luz Esteban (2014, 72) in relation to Women's Houses, because they would also be of use as regards the bertso world, looking ahead:

> As regards the knowledge that emerges in any feminist space [let us imagine feminist spaces in the bertso world], how does it reach, how does it transform, how does it influence, how is it projected in society [let us imagine the bertso world] or other spaces? How are translations of concepts, ideas, theories, practices being carried out? How are power relations among the different feminists, groups, and spaces being administered? Are their connecting spaces, connecting women, connecting positions?

To what point is this knowledge being translated into concrete political actions?

I will leave the questions in the air in the hope that we may answer them collectively.

Bibliography

Agirre Dorronsoro, Lorea. 2010. "Zapia eta txapela Emakume bert-solariak tradizioarekinnegoziatzen eta eredu berria sortzen Negoziazioak eta disonantziak:mututasunetik emulaziora, eta emulaziotik ahots propiora." Master's Thesis, Mondragon University.

Alberdi, Uxue. 2010. "Ezin dut bertsolari izan emakume feministaren kontzientziarik

Gabe." Interview with Ainhoa Agirreazaldegi. *Argia*, March 28. At http://www.argia.eus/argia-astekaria/2224/ainhoa-agirreazaldegi.

————. 2014. "Gorputzak, gorpuzkerak eta gorputzaldiak bertsolar-itzan." In *Gorputza eta generoa: Teoria didaktika eta esperientziak*, edited by Gema Lasarte and Amaia Alvarez. Bilbo: UEU.

————. 2015. "'Ez da kasualitatea', esperientzia feminista bat bert-solaritzan." Lecture as part of the course "Jai ereduak genero ikuspegitik: begirada antropologiko bat Euskal Herriko er-realitateari." UEU, Eibar, July 16.

Alkaiza Guallar, Saioa. 2014. "Bertso eguna, saio deserosoa." *Argia*, January 27. At http://www.argia.eus/albistea/bertso-eguna-saio-deserosoa (las accessed April 12, 2018).

Biglia, Barbara. 2007. "Desde la investigación-acción hacia la inves-tigación activista feminista." In *Perspectivas y retrospectivas de la Psicología Social en los albores del siglo XXI*, edited by José Romay Martínez. Madrid: Biblioteca Nueva.

Bourdieu, Pierre. 1998. *Les Règles de l'art. Genèse et structure du champ litté-raire*. Point Essais. Paris: Seuil.

Del Valle Murga, Teresa. 2012. "Un ensayo metodológico sobre la mirada en la Antropología Social." *Gazeta de Antropología* 28, no. 3. At http://digibug.ugr.es/bitstream/handle/10481/22979/GA%2028-3-10%20TeresadelVallel.pdf?sequence=6&isAllowed=y.

Eizagirre, Estitxu. 2004. "Maritxu, nondik zatoz?" Bertsowoman II Conference, June. At https://www.bertsozale.eus/eu/generoa/dokumentazioa/artikuluak/2004-06-00%20Estitxu%20Eizagirre-%20Maritxu%20nondik%20zatoz.pdf (last accessed April 13, 2018).

———. 2008. "Konplexu eta estereotipoak hausteko ordua." *Erdiko Kaiera* supplement, *Argia*, November 11, 23–26. At http://www.argia.eus/astekaria/docs/2136/pdf/p23-26.pdf (last accessed April 13, 2018).

Ellakuriaga, Izaskun. 1995. "Arantzazu Loidi: Bertso Eskolako Lehen Emaitza." Bertsolari 17 (Spring): 39–41.

Enbeita Maguregi, Onintza. 2016. "Eta hala ere plazan gaude." In *Festak, generoharremanak eta feminismoa. Begirada teoriko eta antropologikoak, praktika sortzaileak eta plazeraren kudeaketa kolektiboak*, edited by Miren Guilló Arakistain. Bilbo: UEU.

Epelde, Edur, Miren Aranguren, and Iratxe Retolaza. 2015. *Gure genealogia feministak. Euskal Herriko mugimendu feministaren kronika bat*. Bilbo: Emagin.

Erkiaga, Nere. 2008. "Genero ikuspegia Bertsolaritzaren mugimendu barruan." Master's Thesis, University of the Basque Country.

Esteban, Mari Luz. 2004a. *Antropología del cuerpo. Género, itinerarios corporales, identidad y cambio*. Barcelona: Edicions Bellaterra.

———. 2004b. "Antropología encarnada. Antropología desde una misma." *Papeles del CEIC* 12 (June): 1–21.

———. 2014. "El feminismo vasco y los circuitos del conocimiento: el movimiento, la universidad y la casa de las mujeres." In *Otras formas de (re)conocer: Reflexiones, herramientas y aplicaciones* desde *la investigación feminista* , edited by Irantzu Mendia Azkue. Donostia-San Sebastián: Hegoa.

————. 2017. *Feminismoa eta politikaren eraldaketak.* Zarautz: Susa.

Etxeberri, Karine. 2015. "'Je sais faire des bertso, mais je ne suis pas bertsolari' Le genre des improvisations chantées au Pays Basque en question." Master's Thesis, Bordeaux Montaigne University.

Euskal Irrati Telebista and Euskal Herriko Bertsozale Elkartea. 2005. *Hitzetik Hortzera.* Television Show. Episode with Ainhoa Agirreazaldegi, May 8. Transcript at https://www.bertsozale. eus/eu/generoa/dokumentazioa/artikuluak/2005-05-08%20 Bertsolaritza%20eta%20emakumea%20-%20Hitzetik%20 Hortzera.pdf.

Garzia, Joxerra, Jon Sarasua, and Andoni Egaña. 2001. *The Art of Bertsolaritza: Improvised Basque Verse Singing.* Donostia: Bertsolari Liburuak.

Goenaga Lizaso, Eider. 2017. "Belaunaldi berria betaurreko moreak jantzita dator." *Gipuzkoako Hitza*, September 8. Interview with Amaia Agirre. At http://gipuzkoa.hitza.eus/2017/09/08/belaunaldi-berria-betaurreko-moreak-jantzita-dator/ (last accessed April 12, 2018).

Haraway, Donna. 1991. "Conocimientos situados: la cuestión científica en el feminismo y el privilegio de la perspectiva parcial." In *Ciencia, cyborgs y mujeres: la reinvención de la naturaleza.* Madrid: Cátedra.

Hérnandez, Jone M. 1999. "Auto/biografía. Auto/etnografía. Auto/retrato." *Ankulegi: gizarte antropologia aldizkaria.* Special edition, *Antropología feminista: desafíos teóricos y metodológicos*: 53–62.

————. 2006. "Emakume bertsolariak: ahozkatu gabeko identitatea." *Kobie. Antropología Cultural* 12: 61–70.

————. 2011a. "Bertsolarismo. Palabras que emocionan, emociones hechas palabras, Incorporaciones antropológicas: Análisis desde el cuerpo y las emociones." Paper presented at XII

Congreso de Antropología de la FAAEE (Federación de Aso-
ciaciones de Antropología del Estado español), León.

―――. 2011b. "Bertsolaritza, definizio berri baterantz?" *Emakunde
aldizkaria* 81: 2–3. At
http://www.emakunde.euskadi.eus/u72-publicac/eu/contenidos/
informacion/sen_revista/eu_emakunde/adjuntos/revista_pa-
pel_81_eu.pdf.

―――. 2016. "Odolak badu generorik? Edo zergatik gorputz emeak
ez diren bertsoetarako bizitoki." In *Etnografia feministak Euskal
Herrian. XXI. mendera begira dagoen antropología*, edited by María
Luz Esteban and Jone M. Hernández García. Bilbo: Udako
Euskal Unibertsitatea and Euskal Herriko Unibertsitatea.

Ibarguren, Leire. 2009. "Emakumeak, oholtza eta umorea." Master's
Thesis, University of the Basque Country. At https://www.
bertsozale.eus/eu/fitxategiak/generoa-dokumentazioa/2009-
leire-ibarguren-emakumeak-oholtza-eta-umorea.

Ibargutxi, Felix. 2017. "Hilean behin biltzen gara emakume bertsolari-
iak, elkarri laguntzeko." Interview with Nerea Ibarzabal. *El
Diario Vasco*, October 14. At http://www.diariovasco.com/cul-
turas/nerea-ibarzabal-bertsolaria-20171014003852-ntvo.html
(last accessed April 12, 2018).

Ibarzabal, Nerea. 2016. "Bertso eguna 2016: bertso-ikuskizuna
eta genero-ikuspegia." Undergraduate Thesis, University
of the Basque Country. At https://addi.ehu.es/bitstream/
handle/10810/18970/NereaIbarzabalSalegui_GRAL.
pdf?sequence=1&isAllowed=y (Last accessed April 12, 2018).

Labaka, Ane. 2017. "Bertsolaritzan garatutako umorea(k) aztergai,
genero ikuspegitik." Master's Thesis, University of the Basque
Country.

Laborde, Denis. 2005. *La mémoire et l'instant: les improvisations chantées du
bertsulari basque*. Donostia and Baiona : Elkar.

Larrañaga, Carmen. 1994. "El Bertsolarismo: habitat de la masculini-
dad." *Bitarte* 4: 29–51.

————. 1997. "Del bertsolarismo silenciado." *Jentilbaratz* 6: 57–73.

Latasa, Zaira. 2010. "Bertsolaria ez da bertsolari jaiotzen, izatera iristen da; Emakumearen ibilbidea bertsolaritzan zehar (1980–2009)." Master's Thesis, University of the Basque Country.

Lujanbio, Maialen. 2007. "Bertsolaritza emakumearen ikuspuntutik: bertsolaritza eta emakumea." Lecture as part of the "Bertso Kritika" (Bertso Critique) initiative by the bertso schools, Orereta, May 11.

Picaza Gorrotxategi, Maitane. 2017. "Espacios propios para las mujeres y procesos de empoderamiento: La Red de Escuelas de Empoderamiento de Bizkaia." Ph.D. diss. University of Deusto.

Piedra, Dabi. 2017. "Zazpi aulki jokoan." *Deia*, October 31. At http://www.deia.eus/2017/10/31/ortzadar/zazpi-aulki-jokoan (last accessed April 12, 2018).

Young, Kate. 2006. "El potencial transformador en las necesidades prácticas: empoderamiento colectivo y el proceso de planificación." In Antología preparada para el Primer Curso Diplomado en desarrollo humano local, género, infancia, población y salud, edited by Reina Fleitas Ruíz and Miguel Márquez. La Habana: Universidad de La Habana-Universitas/Cuba-PNUD/PDHL.

Zabala, Begoña. 2008. *Movimiento de mujeres, mujeres en movimiento*. Tafalla: Txalaparta.

Zelaia, Izarne. 2015. "Emakumeek jendaurreko jardunetan parte hartzeko gaitasunak eskura ditzaten eskolak jokatzen duen papera, bertsolaritza aztergai hartuta." Undergraduate Thesis, University of the Basque Country.

Zinkunegi Barandiaran, Izaro. 2015. "Emakumeak eta bertsolaritza. Gaiak, rolak eta bertsoak genero-ikuspuntutik." *Uztaro* 94: 91–112.

CHAPTER 5

The Presence of Women Bertsolaris as a Kind of Historical Comeback (After Their Eviction from the Public Space)

Larraitz Ariznabarreta

It is well known that on occasion of the Lizardi Prize Contest for improvisational poetry held in Zarautz in 1992, Maialen Lujanbio,[1] in response to Joxerra Garzia's request for a rhyming verse around the topic "It would be great to know who you are," retorted: "As Old Txirrita's only niece I wish I could convey his energy but I still have a lot to learn." If only in a metaphoric manner, the little fib that Lujanbio told on introducing herself—since, as we know, she is not a direct relative of the former Txirrita,[2] despite the fact that

---

1   Maialen Lujanbio was the first woman to win the Bertsolaritza Championship
     in 2009. She won the National Bertsolari Championship for the second time
     in 2017.
2   Txirrita was the nickname given to the master bertsolari Jose Manuel Lujanbio
     (1860–1936), who is regarded as an icon of the traditional bertsolari (belonging
     to the world of orality – a person that improvised bertsos with a specific
     function anywhere (with their importance evaluated later); as opposed to the
     bertsolari from the world of writing – a person that demonstrates, by means

they both share the same last name and birthplace—does contribute to our getting a glimpse into Maialen's references in her beginnings as a junior bertsolari. In fact, I quote the words she used when she was interviewed by Uxue Alberdi for *Argia* (Alberdi 2017):

> Never [have I experienced the subjugation brought about by the fact of being a woman] in a conscious manner. It's rather a notion that I have developed through time in an *a posteriori* manner. My feelings, conscience, and distress as a Basque person came about earlier in time. It's something I have endured since I was a child. My experiences as a bertsolari woman in the public agora were revealed to me later on. Only after years had elapsed did I realize that they run pretty parallel to each other, or at least when it comes to explaining them, they are interchangeable among them.

Hence, Lujanbio's inspiration sources regarding bertsolaritza did not emerge from the theorization of feminism she was to reach later on, nor from the inborn conscience of the difficulties that being a woman brings about. Her first spur came from the traditional bertsolaritza—admittedly male-gendered—and, as the complement thereof, the training through bertso-schooling.[3]

---

of a special performance before a specific audience, their *ability* or *art* when it comes to improvising bertsos). Joxerra Garzia terms as "Great Divide" the (all too) categorical split between written and oral poetry as the "Great Divide." I agree with Garzia in that one should conceive of a continuum rather than a divide between the two taxonomies; at least as a means of examining the issue appropriately. Therefore, here I understand the route from oral to written poetry as "one and the same," embracing the words of Garzia himself that it is like "a progressive grading of phenomena and manifestations of differing degrees of orality, in which there is much overlapping between genres and a fair degree of fusion between orality and writing." See Garzia (2007, 145).

3   In the opinion of Alfredo Retortillo and Xabier Aierdi (2007, 21), as regards bertsolaritza, "its success lies in renewal, not in 'purity'." In this sense, the main achievement of *bertsogintza* (bertso work) has been its ability to incorporate modern characteristics without breaking with tradition. That ability is inherent to bertsolaritza, as a "means of communication," and these researchers study the evolution of vocality in the context of changing balances of power. In their opinion, "*bertsolaritza* has all the accoutrements of present-day global culture, which understands itself only in terms of permanent reformulation" (2007, 20). Specifically, thanks to the hegemonic position bertsolaritza has gained in Basque society, the multiple perspectives in society about bertsogintza are complementary (tradition, popular culture, art, and so on). Likewise, that privileged position has facilitated a seamless continuum with the past.

Gema Lasarte (2016, 168) conducted research subsided by Emakunde (The Basque Institute for Women, dependent of the Basque Autonomous Government), which revealed similar results: the reference frame and imagery of bertsolaritza has changed in the last twenty-five years. In the 1980s, the patterns of bertsolaritza were male-gendered, and even though Kristina Mardaras and Arantzazu Loidi were already onstage, these pioneer women bertsolaris never reached the category of referents.

Therefore, in the period under scrutiny here, and almost up to the present day, bertsolaritza failed to regard women as active subjects—protagonists—or canonical referents. On the contrary, they appear as passive goads and love objects molded by and conforming to men's ideals: there is indeed a difference between being a referred-to object and being the begetter of such referents. There come to mind such bertsos as Xenpelar's "Andre txarraren bentajak" (sic: "The advantages of wicked women") or Txirrita's Neskazar gaztia" (sic: "The young spinster"); but, as we know, those are not the only ones. The meta-narrative forms of traditional bertsolaritza thus represented woman as excluded from their canons until the beginning of twenty-first century. It was not until society, and, of course, the realm of bertsolaritza (in that order, not the opposite), was interpreted from the viewpoint of gender that what we regard a historic truth was accepted: namely, that women are to be accredited with the earliest documented bertso practice in the Middle Ages. Consequently, modern oral improvisation theories have caused today's bertso lady-poets—young and graceful as they are—to reemerge from the depths of history, reporting their appearance on stage as a comeback chronicle.

In its Origins, Were there *Also* Women, or Were They the *Only* Bertsolaris?

Ted Gioia, a historian, music researcher, and university professor, gives in his book *Love Songs: the Hidden History* (2015) some clues that encourage us to undertake further steps to probe the evolution of

women bertsolaris. According to Gioia's research, society is indebted
to women for their lyrical practice and performance of love songs,
and, likewise, for their important contributions to this sort of song.
However, similarly to what happened with bertsolaritza, the forces
of power secured through culture brought about an involution from
the Middle Ages onward, and such sinful practices were taken for
devil's songs, while the music bands led by the ruling class—and,
naturally, the established morale—were granted legitimacy in men's
voices (Gioia 2015a, 48). Love songs, too, as was the case with
bertsolaritza, were denied social visibility insofar as they were not
accepted into the power space.

Following Gioia's logic we can take a further step and assign
the lack of prestige associated with the men-made bertsolaritza to
the above very fact—and, in our case, this adds up to the want of
prestige of Basque language: namely, that men adapted their sing-
ing manner to the way women were wont to sing and, due to the
historic conscience of such a gender/genre change, such a practice
was confronted with criticism and interdiction. Thus, even though
it might sound contradictory, the first steps of the paradigmatic
prestige of bertsolaritza, which is the subject of our analysis, were
based on, and coincided with, the neglect that bertsolaritza was basi-
cally a female activity, which happened a few years before women's
onstage resurgence came about.

Below I quote Gioia's statement on the occasion of an interview
regarding the abovementioned book.

> Yet close study of the cultural evolution of romantic
> music reveals that women contributed most of the key
> innovations in the love song. Even when men took most
> of the credit—which often happened—they frequently
> constructed their songs by imitating the earlier works of
> female singers. To some extent, the history of the love
> song can be described as the process of men learning to
> sing as if they were women. In many times and places, this
> gender shift has led to criticism, and sometimes prohibi-
> tion (Gioia 2015b).

The concealed history Gioia means to underscore does not only concern love songs, or women's roles themselves. Nevertheless, the tendency is quite widespread: the coarse and uncouth productions of those subdued would soon become a part of the refined cultural wealth of rulers, robbing the authentic protagonists of their merit and worth.

Women Bertsolaris Toward Referentiality

The (re)appearance of women bertsolaris that has taken place in recent years and which is our aim to recall, through the synecdochic figure of Maialen Lujanbio, has undergone different stages, as well as obstacles: Miren Artetxe's mention of the glass ceiling in the latest Championship—repeated fairly often thereafter— was not a mere pun, as has been proved. Rather than having us collect a medley of such hindrances, they have been much better gathered in the plentiful interviews carried out with the protagonists, and have been the central issue of so many research works too.[4] For our purposes here, I find it sufficient to make a summary of such challenges and accomplishments.

The lack of women's visibility and referentiality opened up a path to some sporadic, odd, and symbolic representations in the early years. Thus, Maialen Lujanbio's "txapela" championship in 2009 was held by many as the triumph of "all women bertsolaris;" and, likewise, every onstage appearance by Estitxu Arozena, Ainhoa Agirreazaldegi, and Uxue Alberdi—not to mention but three leader-icons—are felt as symbols or tokens of all bertsozale women's empowerment. But even if such an embodiment can hardly be regarded as an expression of women's subjugation, it will at least be easily understood as an extra burden laid on the head of the icons (bertsolaris). Being the icon of an idea or group does bring along a commitment to comply with external requirements, besides one's self-requirements, personal limits, and boundary markers: that is to say, a sort of exercise moving from *one*self to *other*self. Maialen

---

4   For a closer examination of the bibliography related to the topic, see the reference section in Lasarte et al. (2016).

Lujanbio (2007) herself owns up to experiencing difficulties in the exercise of such identity shifts.

> Being someone else's creativity proxy is not appealing at all, but is pretty much a hurdle to one's inspiration. It is better to have a choice rather than to appoint a person the representative of the whole group.

Therefore, bertsolaris have also set a target in diversity with regards to women bertsolaris' representation. In such a process, along with many a bertsolari who has joined in the theorization of feminism, women bertsolaris have also set up their own steads here and there, with the aim of turning them into domains of liberty.

Earlier on, in 2009, the Bertsozale Elkarteak entity included a gender section in its institutional structure, thus making it possible to gather the emotions and identities that go beyond the members' biological sex as reflected in their curricula, whether they pertained to a bertso school or a summercamp bertso school. Nevertheless, while there is an obvious male hegemony and the quantitative female presence is still a challenge, there are those who see the issue as something that surpasses figures. The bertsolari Jon Maia, having granted that the gender issue is a structural matter, went on to make the following reflection to Gorka Erostarbe (2018) in *Berria*:

> I would not make a categorization by sexes; a man or male gender person, for example, can have a deep sensibility or conscience, while a woman may not have developed it so much. The sexual organs of the leading six or eight bertsolaris onstage shouldn't be a criterion to assess the gender presence. If we started analyzing each person's attitude and sensibility, the task wouldn't be as simple as that, just as it isn't easy to probe the identity of a man or a woman.

Modern Bertsolaritza in the Direction of Acme Ideology

Leaving aside efforts to make quantitative and exhaustive appraisals, we can also get a general panoramic view of the process. The found backbone of recent times up to the present lies in the Bertso Elkartea association and the network of bertso schools. They both deserve a heedful exploration of their genesis, development, and current state, but we will take for granted that we are sufficiently acquainted with their essence and the connection between the above two instances, which is unquestionably the drive of contemporary bertsolaritza. For the purpose of this work we will call it bertsogunea (the realm of bertsos).

Bertsogunea has, thus, thanks to its social wholeness, drawn up its pathway with a rejuvenating and modernizing thrust. Along with it, there is a well-stocked multiplicity of personal and performative styles among bertsolaris, but always keeping themselves within the boundaries marked by the renewed old ideological predominant orthodoxy. In this process, women's gradual achievement of a well-deserved place in bertsolaritza is the most noteworthy aspect and, undoubtedly, the most important one. Misogynistic institutions and attitudes are well aware that things will never abide by the old patterns once women have settled in and been granted the right to stay. That is why women must acquiesce entry even if, fairly often, that entails breaking chains or knocking over doors.

Such strife or toil might have yielded a harsh situation in bertsolaritza, bearing in mind what and where the starting-point in previous times was, namely, a world packed with all kinds of female traditional stereotypes. Luckily, the perspectives and values that gradually emerged within the ideological sphere had already been assumed by the modern youth in bertsogune, and being an icon in the new times implied relinquishing male-chauvinism, misogyny, and homophobia while embracing feminism, at least in its general discourse, as in society. Thus, it has gradually, step by step, become gender-inclusive and from the perspective of modernity, it has also elaborated and polished the very discourse about gender.

There is another ailing topic that deserves a special mention. Indeed, as the Basque intelligentsia approached bertsolaritza, it meant to refine it and bestow some prestige on it, and indeed, as time and history went on bertsolaritza has acquired such prestige and dignity, this being its main purpose, in principle at least, to prevail as the best passport for all other intellectual and artistic works to rise to the highest place. Noteworthy, in this respect, there is a list of bertsolari champions who have traveled a long path in other spheres: Amuriza, Egaña, Arzallus, Lujanbio, and so on. And even with not so renowned names, we can also make a long list of bertsolaris who have taken up the place of Basarri in journalism,[5] the latter going from the omnipresence of Xabier Euzkitze to the humbler opinion columnists in Basque newspapers. We might think that the abilities and gifts bertsolaris are endowed with turn out handy in whichever field. On the one hand, this should come as no surprise, since even in adjacent territories, being in the media is the shortest, fastest, and safest way of climbing up the social ladder

In university and scholarly research. too, Basque improvisational poetry is becoming one of the most gripping subject matters of late, assigning it a relationship with everything and anything in whichever manner and field. It seems that there, again, a circle has been closed: traditional canonical poets like Lizardi, Lauaxeta, and others alike turned out to be aloof to grassroots people, and bertsolaris strove to "poeticize" the old Basque intelligentsia; whereas new bertsolaritza has put the very academy itself at its service, with the conviction that it is the only way and the least exhausting method to endow it with a Basque culture label.

Once this stage has been reached, a competition has been building up as to who will be more effective in driving forward bertsogune's renewed ideology, its pathway, and on what terms.

---

5   According to Garzia (2007, 147), the mental categories used by contemporary bertsolaris and writers are very similar: "Perhaps this also explains," he continues, "the abundance and success of so many bertsolaris as newspaper columnists."

As gender discourse goes beyond women's presence and demand for equal opportunities, the ambiguity of gender and sex-role are subjects of discussion onstage. We quote below Maialen Lujanbio's resounding verse about this topic:

> I'm a man and a woman
> neither a man nor a woman;
> will perchance my desire not to be anywhere
> induce your restlessness?

It could be the case that the audience as a whole does not agree with this new viewpoint and discourse (or, more doubtlessly, that the traditional audiences do not apprehend it, or that they hardly care about new modern discourses, give or take a certain rhetoric "restlessness"), but the hegemony of bertsogunea and the accolade it is greeted with would suffuse any kind of grimace.[6]

Sociology has long since studied the *ethos* caused on rituals by group protection and how the agenda can affect individual behaviour. The French sociologist Durkheim, in his research on Central Australia's aborigines, discovered the sacred character of cultural symbols and, hence, perceived that these totems were nothing but formal symbolic prompts in native people's rituals: aborigines worshipped themselves and their communal structures when socially binding together.

Bibliography

Alberdi, Uxue. 2017. "Euskaratik eta gure mundu erreferentzialetik egin behar dugu, besteen ispiluetan gure buruaren bila ibili gabe." *Argia*, March 14. At https://www.argia.eus/albistea/eu-

---

6   My aim being not to conceal anything, there is one trait peculiar to bertso performances that I consider deserves some insight: the unwritten law: *txalo beti eta txistu inoiz ez* (let there be always applause and never any booing). How come? Is it that there is never a bad or ominous bertso brought on stage? Is it that microphones are snatched from those prone to utter uncalled-for locutions? In that sense, there would be an analogy not with sports, but with rituals. The competition between bertsolaris is held back by the group performances: they are all applause-deserving champions, including the public.

skaratik-eta-gure-mundu-erreferentzialetik-egin-behar-dugu-
besteen-ispiluetan-gure-buruaren-bila-ibili-gabe.

Durkheim, Emile. 1912; 1965. *The Elementary Forms of the Religious Life.*
New York: Free Press, New York.

Erostarbe, Gorka. 2018. "Bertsoaren barruko edukia erabat aldatu
da." *Berria*, February 11. At https://www.berria.eus/al-
bisteak/148819/bertsoaren_barruko_edukia_erabat_aldatu_
da.htm.

Garzia, Joxerra. 2007. "Toward True Diversity in Frame of Reference."
Oral Tradition 22, no. 2: 143–56.

Gioia, Ted. 2015a. *Love Songs: The Hidden History.* New York: Oxford
University Press.

———. 2015b. "The Love Song and its Complex Gender His-
tory." *Oxford University Press' Academic Insights for the Thinking
World. OUP Blog* (February 12). Available at: https://blog.oup.
com/2015/02/love-song-complex-gender-history/.

Lasarte, Gema, et.al. 2016. *Emakume bertsolariak: ahanzturatik diskurtso
propiora. Hegemonikoki gizonezkoa izan den eremura emakumeen hur-
bilketa ahalbideratu duten iniziatiba eta faktoreen azterketa.* Vitoria-
Gasteiz: Emakunde. At http://www.emakunde.euskadi.eus/
contenidos/informacion/publicaciones_subvencionadas2/
eu_def/adjuntos/beca.2015.2.emakume_bertsolariak.pdf.

Lujanbio, Maialen. 2007. "Bertsolarien arteko amildegia." *Argia*, July 3.
At https://www.argia.eus/albistea/bertsolarien-arteko-amilde-
gia-u-iturriaga-j-montero-eta-m-lujanbio?ids=albistea/bertso-
larien-arteko-amildegia-u-iturriaga-j-montero-eta-m-lujanbio.

Retortillo, Alfredo, and Xabier Aierdi. 2007. "A Sociological Study of
Sung, Extempore Verse-Making in Basque." *Oral Tradition* 22,
no. 2: 13–31.

CHAPTER 6

What is the Sex of a Bertsolaria?

Joseba Zulaika

There is no other domain of experience in which Basque society has run into cultural impasses as distressing as gender. A case in point is the ritualized performances of the *alardes* in Irun and Hondarribia—annual festival parades that celebrate a 1639 military victory against the French army and in which traditionally only men took part as armed soldiers while women were left to participate as the *cantinera* (serving girl), one token of female presence for each company composed of more than a hundred men. When feminists demanded to take part as soldiers in 1996 and later organized an alternative alarde, a perplexing crisis ensued with ferocious arguments on both sides either affirming or questioning the legitimacy of the traditional parade, leading to violent clashes between the two sides; the demand to change a ritual ceremony that mixes tradition, festivity, and gender roles became for both sides a source of outrage and violence that affected every household in both towns. The commotion keeps repeating annually with apparently no available negotiation between the two antagonistic sides. The gender impasse could hardly be acted out in more dramatic terms.

Bertsolaritza singing traditionally took place in bars and plazas; it was a public performance that belonged to the male domain; it was rare that a woman would sing in public—despite the fact that there are instances, since the fifteenth century, of bertsoak being sung by women (Larrañaga 1995). When bertso singing became part of the curriculum in Basque schools on the 1980s and 1990s, and girls started singing along with the boys, the typical bertsolaria performance was no longer only a men's affair, as reflected in the participation of the various types of competitive bertso championships. During the 2005 national bertsolaria championship, which takes place every four years, 25 of the 150 participants (15 percent) were women; by 2013, their participations went up to 41 out of the 191 participants (21 percent) (Astiz 2013). In 2009 Maialen Lujanbio was the only woman among the eight finalists; in a memorable day in the history of bertsolaria competitions, she won the *txapela* (beret) that signals the national champion. In 2013 Oihane Perea won the provincial championship of Araba. And then again in December 2017 Maialen Lujanbio won the national championship with a performance that was unanimously deemed to be above the rest.

"Championship" is referred to in Basque as *txapelketa*—which could be translated as "in search of the txapela." The winner of the competition is honored with a large txapela on which the word "champion" and the date is engraved. The Basque traditional txapela is a flat, wide, single seamless piece made of natural wool, without a peak, the surrounding section folded inside. It is worn almost exclusively by men on a daily basis. So there was some gender collision when Lujanbio, a young woman bertsolaria just declared champion, grabbed this most typically male headgear for everyone to see. As if to emphasize the symbolic dissonance and further destabilize the prevalence of the male symbol, in her farewell bertso strophes and while wearing the txapela of the champion, Lujanbio invoked a different headwear, the *gobara* (a cloth women used to put on their heads to carry the laundry) that belonged to the generations of her mothers and grandmothers. Her song brought together the traditional female head cover she was invoking and the male beret she was wearing. The overall result was that the very maleness of the txapela, its strong cultural character, was compromised in Lujambio's head. Indeed, one might ask what was the *sex* of Lujambio's txapela. The perplexed audience would have been at pains to find an adequate reply.

But it was not the symbolism of the headwear that was Lujanbio's principal message in her farewell bertso. It was the relevance of *Euskara* (also spelled Euskera), the Basque language, that was her axiomatic statement and the true source of power and enjoyment. In a memorable bertso that sounded like a manifesto she summed up thus her audience's ultimate desire as Basque speakers:

> This evening we return
> to the four corners of the Basque Country.
> And with the energy, passion, and
> heartbeats of joy gathered here
> let us keep recreating our country
> from the Euskara and in Euskara.

Lujanbio's bertso was both a proclamation that Euskara is the central *event* around which Basques had to reaffirm their historical identity as well as an invitation to recreate a new Basque society propelled by the force of a deeply shared communal song and a new feminism. She was singing this song in a building, the Bilbao Exhibition Center, that had recently emerged from the ruins of the *Altos Hornos* (Tall Ovens) ironworks and in a Basque city, Bilbao, in which Euskara is mostly unspoken. "Euskara" was language, identity, bond, mission, sacrament—was the axiom of the new Basque community proclaimed by Lujanbio, her song presided over by two at first sight conflicting symbols, the male *txapela* and the female *gobara*.

The audience at BEC was overtaken by the evidence of a historic shift whose meanings and implications were obvious and yet hard to articulate. The event of Lujanbio being proclaimed as the best singer in 2009 is a clear signal that a new female subjectivity has emerged in bertsolaritza. Judging from the reactions of the public, and in particular from those of her seven male bertsolaria competitors, first hugging her profusely, then standing behind her with their arms entwined on their shoulders, it was clear that Lujanbio's txapela was experienced by men as well as women as a singular event that implied a historic breakthrough in the history of bertsolaritza, a cultural phenomenon that could find echoes in the history of Basque resistance and linguistic revival. In December 2017 that historic event was repeated when Lujanbio again won the txapela.

We therefore have to ask: what exactly is this historic breakthrough? The question forces on us an investigation of the relationship between bertsolaritza and gender. If sexuality is attached to the (male) txapela, is it to the "mother tongue" Euskara, and perhaps to the bertso song itself, and to the bertsolaria as a performing subject as well. What actually is the sex of the bertsolaria? What is his/her true source of satisfaction?

Am I a Man or a Woman?
Cultural Models and the Hystericized Bertsolaria

The bertsolaria who put the txapela on Lujanbio's head in 2009 was an eighty-year-old man, Joxe Agirre, a traditional family man who lived all his life in a rural setting as sheepherder and farmer. Lujanbio was at the time thirty-three, single, and college educated. Both of them shared the same formal art of bertsolaritza and had been singing partners on many occasions. The affection between the two of them was palpable when he put the txapela on her head and in their subsequent farewell bertso strophes praising each other. And yet, the two of them could not have been more different in their cultural, political, and subjective outlooks. The presence of Joxe Agirre underscored the starkness of the transition from the traditional type of male versifying to the new generational one, open to all kinds of experiments and hybrid forms in its various ideological and sexual forms.

In one of her interviews Lujanbio pointed out that bertsolaritza is not for her only a formal-aesthetic performance, that she also wanted to express her own subjective voice. What could be this new voice, this new subjectivity? A reverse way of asking the same question is: what are the impasses that make the traditional male song incapable of going any further? Or we might also ask: what type of "man" was Lujanbio on that stage when she was singing her farewell bertso dressed in the men's txapela and invoking the women's gobara? As remarked earlier, Lujanbio's first act of hybridization affected the txapela itself. From the beginning she established a dialectical image of complementarity and opposition between the txapela and the gobara, and in doing so she hybridized the txapela and deprived it from its being the *only* (male) reigning headwear. At the same time she was suddenly the "man" by having won the txapela in a hard-fought competition, and yet she was as much the "woman" with the gobara of all her past and present generations of women.

The mixing of genders and the hybridization of symbols poses, in psychoanalytic terms, the issue of the sexual identity of the bertsolaria and the basic question that produces hysteria: Am I a man or a woman? (Is my desire as a woman my own, or is it a reflection of what man wants me to desire?) Standing here on the stage as a woman while wearing a txapela, am I man or a woman? Is my desire as a bertsolaria my own, or is it what the bertso public, that voracious Master, wants me to desire? Historical narratives that have created men's roles have to do with the discourses of wars, adventures, sports, competition, whereas historically a relevant language spoken by women, reduced to silence, has been the one of the hysterical body.

In the context of the bertsolaria championship we should ask to what extent are both men and women hystericized. The hysterical deadlock emerges when the symbolic identity a subject is given (say, "champion") does not correspond to his/her actual psychological reality and begins questioning or feeling discomfort with such identity. One remembers Andoni Egaña declaring before his last championship in 2009 that he would be happier if not him but someone else would end up wearing the txapela the day of the competition—it seems he had grown uncomfortable with his repeated role as champion. Lujanbio, who was second in 2005, was said to have replied to an interviewer that she preferred not to win—as if she did not think she was herself ready yet for such a high role. In the bertso championship of 1936, Uztapide and Txirrita tied after a day of singing —a rare event in any sport that seeks to produce a winner and a loser. A very young Uztapide, even if he was reportedly told that he was the actual winner, preferred to defer the txapela to the great Txirrita with the argument that he had enough time in the future to win again—the young man felt uncomfortable being proclaimed champion over the legendary Txirrita.

Such difficulty in accepting one´s own symbolic identity is called in psychoanalytic literature the hysterical impasse. This type of deadlock is summed up in Jenny Holzer's famous strip: "Protect me from what I want." These impasses extend to areas such as language, culture, arts, politics, and sexuality. A woman saying "protect me from my desire" might be interpreted as begging to the male benevolent patriarchal figure, "don't let me self-destruct." But more radically it can be read

> as pointing towards the fact that in today's patriarchal society, woman's desire is radically alienated: she desires what men expect her to desire, desires to be desired by men. In this case, 'Protect me from what I want' means: "Precisely when I seem to express my authentic innermost longing, 'what I want' has already been imposed on me by the patriarchal order that tells me what to desire, so the first condition of my liberation is that I break the vicious cycle of my alienated desire and learn to formulate my desire in an autonomous way" (Zizek 2000, 38–39).

Eagerness to play the next game is what you expect from a sports man or woman. Xabier Amuriza defined bertsolaritza as "the national sport." And yet, you will not find many bertsolariak who are eager to participate in a bertso championship. The usual thing you hear from them is how tough and nerve-wrecking such competitions are, but they do participate as an obligation to please their bertsolaria public. By turning a verbal play into a competitive game, the championship ends up hystericizing the bertsolaria. Echoing Holzer's strip, my suspicion is that many bertsolariak are silently praying, "Protect me from my bertso fans, protect me from the need to compete, protect me from having to win, protect me from having to make my colleagues losers." The fundamental impasse of human desire is that our desire is the other's desire, both in the sense of desiring the other and, especially, for desiring what the other desires. This forces the bertsolaria to go along with the public's desire for competition. But it easily forces on him or her the question: am I here competing in front of twelve thousand people because I really want to be here or because my public demands that I be here?

Every bertsolaria is likely to have experienced situations of hysterical impasse. There is a remarkable case that happened to Xalbador, a sheepherder considered one of the greatest singers ever, but who had the disadvantage that his French Basque dialect was difficult for the Spanish Basque speakers to understand. In the 1967 championship, at the end of the day the jury chose Uztapide and Xalbador to be the finalists among the eight bertsolaria participants. A section of the public, which was in favor of another bertsolaria, did not like the decision and booed the selection of Xalbador for more than five minutes. Facing that very public right after the booing, Xalbador sang a memorable bertso that is much remembered by the fans: "Brothers and sisters, please don't think I am happy to be here/ I'd prefer to be on the side watching the singers./ If you are not happy with the decision/ it's not my fault. /You have booed me/ but I still love you." He was still in the middle of the strophe when the public was already applauding; when he was finished the public, raised to their feet, went wild cheering the very bertsolaria they had just booed, while Xalbador stood silently crying. In his autobiography (Olaizola 1976) Uztapide deplored the event. He also lamented the anxiety the bertsolariak are thrown into with the occasion of the championships and celebrated the fact that, after the Xalbador incident, future championships were cancelled (they were resumed again in the 1980s). The bertsolaria placed in a competitive context is begging: "Please, don't think I am happy to be here; please don't put me in this impasse." But at the same time we cannot forget the psychoanalytic view by which "for Freud. . . . the hysterical subject is rather a kind of *symptom* of the Master—what he renders palpable is the primordial deadlock that pertains to the dimension of subjectivity as such, and which is concealed by the posture of the Master" (Zizek 1999, 190).

Another solution to such deadlocks suffered by a bertsolaria in a competitive context was that of Jon Sarasua, himself a finalist in the 1986 and 1991 championships. In the middle of a competition in which he was one of the favorites to win, he disqualified all his chances by deliberately singing a bertso that did not follow the usual formal strictures of the song as a sign of rebellion against the championship. This was clear case of hysterical self-sabotage in which his goal was to destroy the very formal rules of the bertso in order to save it from competition.

Artist María José Balbel (See Zilbeti 2016, 149, 153) remarks that one of the critical features of feminist thought is in fact a critical attitude toward the binarism of win/lose. Not surprisingly, one of the issues that emerged in modern bertsolaritza, and which is still a subject of debate, is the dominant role championships play in it as they have turned into the most visual bertso event, and which in a previous essay (Zulaika 1985) I linked to male competitive *joko* (game) roles. Linda Nochlin's well-known question "Why Have There Been No Great Women Artists?" applies poignantly to women bertsolariak as well. In the Basque case the historic reason why there were no great women bertsolariak until recently has to do with the traditional male and females cultural domains. Competitive *joko* games in particular, such as sports and betting, which were performed in the public domain of the plaza, belonged almost exclusively to men. To the extent that bertsolaritza was a public event to take place in bars or plazas, women were excluded from it. If furthermore the bertsolariak were perceived to be singing in a *joko* type of competition, women were further excluded.

The elementary *joko* game has typically a bipolar structure between two competitors, performing on a level playing field with preestablished rules and measurements, and which will clearly result in a winner and a loser. In Basque culture there is an alternative cultural model of performance that is *jolas* "play," which at times seems undistinguishable from *joko*, but which has starkly different cultural premises. In jolas you simply play, as children do for example, although not in order to produce a winner or loser, but mostly for entertainment or fun. If the rules must be well set and literally preserved in competition, in play the rules are mere guides, can be overturned, may in fact be interpreted metaphorically and mean the opposite of their literal meaning, its beginning and ending totally arbitrary. If *joko* results are strict in producing *either* a winner *or* a loser, you could say that *jolas* breaks down the either/ or and results in both sides being simultaneously winners and losers. Gregory Bateson theorizes that the semantics of "this is play" creates a frame presided by the premise: "All the statements within this frame are untrue" (Bateson 1972, 184). If in joko one obtains the literal "truth" of a clear winner by following clearly established rules, in playful interaction words do not have literal meaning and rules are there in part to be broken. "Winning" in jolas or joko has different implications. Even when performing in a joko competitive context the bertsolariak and their fans know that the bertso song is essentially a verbal jolas.

How do sexual roles apply to such a jolas/joko continuum? The translation of these premises to a bertsolaria performance will be, at least initially, detrimental to women; the cultural tendency will push men to perceive a girl among other bertsolariak as an exception to the male public domain. In the competitive context of the championship, a modernization of the traditional joko, now with all the modern media's technological spectacle, and in which the implicit premise used to be that women should not engage in public joko, the cultural tendency will be that she is perceived as taking part in some jolas performance rather than actually competing. The championship itself is obviously changing these perceptions. Lujanbio's victory meant among other things that women were no longer performing just in jolas, as if they were tokens of exception, but could beat men in their own joko. Long perceived cultural premises regarding male/female roles in public competitive arenas had to be revisited. By changing all of that, Lujanbio was empowering

Basque women to see themselves as truly equal to men. Ironically, if the joko championship frame was in the past the realm of men's action, the same joko was now allowing women to demonstrate their true worth by coming up victorious against men and thus the championship was self-defeating its own male bias.

But is this all the transformation that women singers can do within bertsolaritza? Now that they will increasingly prove that they can beat men in the verbal art of improvised bertso, should their participation serve to underpin the joko definition of bertsolaritza? If they did so, would they not essentially replicate the contents of the traditional male subject defined by a literal joko sense of winning and losing? Should they not instead bring the awareness of their female subjectivities to further relativize the joko championship frame as the dominant model of bertsolaritza and remind the public that their art relies far more on the verbal playfulness of jolas? Indeed, a bertso operates though ambiguity and metaphor, that is, through the "lies" of homonymy, humor, hyperbole, and indirection.

For the bertsolaria champion, the txapela he/she wears to signify his/her status as best singer is something added to the bertsolaria and not part of his/her nature. That gap between what one is and what one represents by the addition of a symbolic title is conceptualized in psychoanalysis as "symbolic castration"—it is not really me here but I am symbolically a mask, a mere stand-in for the big Other I represent. "Femininity" as a masquerade is an instance of it; ostentatious "masculinity" is another.

These masks hide the ontological anxiety as to who or what one is—and the urgency of having to *believe* that one is a man or having to *pretend* that one is a woman (Zupancic 2017, 56–57.). Such anxiety has to explain in good part the shocking intensity of the dissonance created by the abovementioned alardes and the ensuing violent reactions. Men's masculinity requires displays such as armed military virility that mask the fear of not having what it takes to be a man, an anxiety that is part of masculine subjectivity as such. The exclusion of women is intrinsic to such affirmation of manhood; if women intrude into traditionally "male" performances (soccer player, soldier, priest), one way to alleviate the anxiety of their intrusion is to ask whether they really are women. The source of the anxiety should be clear: behind these performances and masks

> there is no substantial subjectivity . . . masculinity being but a simulacrum of a substantial subjectivity. When men feel threatened by such women, it is not simply that they represent for them a "threat of castration;" rather, their presence makes it harder for men to sustain the repression of castration; it weakens the defense of anxiety. And this explains the often violent and affect-ridden reactions to these women (Ibid., 57).

The alarde's all-male military parade is an assertion of masculinity's masquerade needed by men to show their manliness vis-à-vis their women; questioning the value of such masquerade and arguing that women also could adopt it can be felt as a mortal threat to masculinity as such, one accepted traditionally by both men and women, hence the violent reaction. In a performance that until recently was mostly a "male" accomplishment, the swift manner in which bertsolariak have allowed the incorporation of women, and have even granted the supreme symbol of excellence, the txapela, to one of them, speaks volumes.

This type of "castration" affects every speaking being, man or woman, in the sense that language is not-whole and splits every subject. The theoretical consequence of this psychoanalytic perspective is articulated thus by Juliet Flower MacCannell (1994, 106–7):

> If the *subject* in psychoanalytical terms is what is "castrated" or divided by language and mobilized into a universe of desire, the presumption that the form of this desire is universal, i.e. phallic, renders woman essentially speechless. Her silence as daughter, her wifely echoing of her man, her professionally "masculine" adoption of male language would seem to be the only channels open to her as she closes off and drowns out her mother's voice. These two options—speechlessness or fully male speech—structure the whole story of woman's speech, of her relation to the signifier.

A similar hysteric position is thrown into the suddenly "feminized" bertsolaria who is left with two options: either not participating in the competitions or else adopting an entirely "male" subject of bipolar competition. This requires a new theoretical outlook coming especially from feminism. The mere presence of women bertsolariak is not enough; the bertso songs themselves must be critical of the patriarchal systems of representation, dynamite them from inside, if a new feminine subjectivity is to emerge for both men and women bertsolariak.

Songs for Nothing: Deadlocks and Breakthroughs

A Basque artist/writer famous for his hysterical impasses and who wrote insightfully about bertsolaritza was the sculptor Oteiza. His entire artistic evolution concluded and was defined by his *endgame* at the pinnacle of his career. Having won one of the most prestigious international awards for sculpture in 1957, he decided to give up sculpture altogether. He explained: "Man defines himself by what he needs: I no longer need my statues, so I am no longer a sculptor" (Oteiza 1963, #89). He was saying, "Protect me from my statues." When he had reached what he had wanted, he felt so uncomfortable with his new symbolic role of the successful international artist that he preferred to give it all up. Oteiza's "hysteria" was in the end a liberating force—from the fetishism of the art at the service of the market and the heroics of the individual genius. A subject confronted with truth becomes hysterical. The Lacanian premise is that "only hysteria produces new knowledge" (Zizek 2017, 4). Oteiza applied to himself the image of the bullfighter entrapped at the center of the plaza: "from this *encierro* I infinitely want to escape," he wrote.

In literature there is the emblematic deadlock in which Beckett found himself in the mid-1950s, unable to write for years and which led him to write *Texts for Nothing* and *Endgame*. In his creative blockage he found it impossible to go on, torn between the solipsistic cogito and the blackness of being (See Badiou 2008, 64). It would take him ten years to get over this impasse (Badiou 2003, 39). How did he succeed in passing from such "for nothing" into the continuation of his work? In Badiou's commentary, "It passed, I am convinced, through a veritable intellectual and artistic mutation, and more precisely through a modification in his *orientation of thought*" (Badiou 2008, 264). I am bringing up here the case of Beckett's breakthrough to ask whether a similar mutation in artistic form and thought might be happening now to the post-patriarchal bertsolaria. Badiou fleshes out Beckett's mutation as one of privileging "what happens" and the encounter with the alterity of the other. The subject is no longer concerned primarily with identity but with occurrences of the subject's possible positions.

And is not the bertsolaria also entrapped in an encierro while standing up on the stage in the middle of the plaza, while trying to give voice to an audience's varied dreams and desires through her own subjectivity, at times successfully, at times engaged in a hopeless effort to challenge the audience into a different kind of subject? One imagines that many times the bertsolaria has to walk down from the stage feeling defeated, robbed from her song, wondering whether the audience really captured the gist of her singing, asking herself whether it is worth continuing to subject herself to such an enormous effort, singing and achieving nothing.

One thing clear to Beckett was that, "success and failure on the public level never mattered much to me, in fact I feel much more at home with the latter" (Quoted in Cronin 1997, 455). He thought it was an illusion to hope that a successful work of art would change things and alleviate the human condition. Badiou argues that "Beckett is a writer of hope, but a hope based on nothing. . . 'Nothing,' because the ultimate resource from which generic humanity draws its cognitive and practical capacity for novelty . . . is the *void*" (Power and Toscano 2003, xxx). Obviously "'nothing' does not constitute a failing, because . . . 'nothing is more real than nothing'" (Badiou 2003, 54).

In the traditional Basque gender stereotypes of the men of older generations, acceptance of the anthropological discourse of the matriarchal regime is no accident; only patriarchal fantasy could have invented such a myth and feminism has been forced to renounce it. Real women should be kept apart from the real manly struggle but they should be there to receive men's life offering. It is about this mysterious, ineffable female essence that Lacan said his famous "Woman does not exist." The political consequences of this absent woman can be seen in writer and political activist Txillardegi's first novel *Leturiaren egunkari ezkutua* (Leturia's secret diary) in which the protagonist sacrifices his love of Miren for the country. Miren is for the men of ETA's generation the archetype of the role of woman in relation to revolutionary action, that is, essentially a stand-in for male political desire, merely a symptom to satiate the male hero's thirst for the Absolute. It would take decades, in Basque literature and politics, before feminism would proclaim the presence of real women who refuse to be reduced to the role of substitutes for a male projection.

Remarking on the existence of gender impasses in Basque culture, I mentioned the case of the alardes and the feminist demand that women participate not only as *cantinera* "exceptions" to the all-male parade but, overturning the traditional gender symbolic structure, that they do so on an equal basis with men. In the case of women bertsolariak, during the bertso championship finals of 2005, 2009, 2013, and 2017, Lujanbio was the only woman, thus replicating the female exception to the all-male universal. What is apparent in the case of the cantinera is that she is chosen to represent feminine beauty, a token of the female sex. To the extent that women bertsolariak were perceived by men and the general public as tokens, the tendency was similarly to relate to them as objects of idealization and seduction, not as real women present with their actual bodies. The recent work by Jone Miren Hernández emphasizes persuasively, beyond the art's ideological and rhetorical components, the central role emotions and bodily experience play in the enjoyment of bertsolaritza (Hernández 2018).

This brings us to the historic change that women's participation has affected in bertsolaritza during the recent years. Women are no longer providers of stereotypical themes for men to sing about, or rare tokens among male singers, or abstractions to be idealized and loved at a distance; women are suddenly real desublimated bodies standing next to men while grabbing a microphone, responding to men's bertso stereotypes and idealizations with their own real situations and perspectives, competing with men in attention and argument and song. I am afraid that, when listening to a berstolaria, we traditional men still feel far more comfortable with sublime women's roles, such as motherhood or sacrificial figures or beauty pageants, than with real women who can speak and make demands or laugh at you.

One imagines that, each time a woman bertsolaria steps up to a stage, it must be difficult for her to address in front of an audience topics that combine the current changing status of politics, gender, and subjectivity. Many of her listeners are members of my generation who are still subjectively closer to premodern types of gender and heroism by which men justified risking everything for a Cause, while women were reduced to the roles of passing errands or being mothers. Such transitions of political subjectivity demanded from older generations have been dramatic in recent years—in relation to ETA, significantly, as well as in relation to the new waves of Europeanization and globalization. Even in ETA feminism was a "most urgent task," Yoyes argued, adding: "What should I do for these men to understand and fully assume that women's liberation is a revolutionary priority?" (Garmendia 1987, 57). What was a revolutionary priority in ETA was clearly a poetic priority in bertsolaritza—not just the presence of women among the bertsolariak but the transformation of the singers' traditional patriarchal subject. Yoyes not only rejected the machismo of her comrades, she was also afraid that she might herself succumb to it: "I don't want to become the woman who is accepted because men consider her in some way macho." When Lujanbio was for years the only woman among bertsolaria men, I wonder to what extent she was expected to behave and argue like a man, and how many times she must have heard that her singing "was not bad for a woman."

What really matters are the changes experienced in the coordinates of one's subjectivity. In order to create a new subject one has to have the courage to take the position that "in the modern ethical constellation . . . one bears witness to one's fidelity to the Thing by sacrificing (also) the Thing itself" (Zizek 2000, 154). This is what Yoyes did with ETA. But it was also what the new generation of artists did with Oteiza and Chillida, as summarized by Txomin Badiola in a workshop whose title revealed the inaugural premise, *Arreglárselas sin el padre* (Getting on Without the Father) (Zulaika 2014, 146). It was the recognition that the Father's position of the big Other is now vacant. The post-Oteizian younger generation of artists showed fidelity to the artistic Thing by sacrificing it, much as many radical Christians kept fidelity to the religious Thing by becoming atheists, and by recreating an Oteiza tailor-made for their own artistic revival.

Similarly, the new generation of bertsolariak finds that the Father's figure is no longer what it was. When Joxe Agirre placed the txapela on Lujanbio's head, despite their using the same formal and musical strictures, there was little doubt that the song of the new generation represented by Lujanbio was subjectively and politically an overturning of Agirre's bertsolaritza. You show fidelity to the bertso Thing by sacrificing the classical subject and arguments of the Thing itself. You persevere in the value of the song by transforming it. As was said of Antigone, "Perseverance does not consist in the repetition of a 'pattern of behavior', but of the performance, in the face of enormous obstacles, of a creative act, and it results not in the preservation of the very core of her being—however wayward or perverse—but of its complete overturning. Antigone's perseverance is not indicated by her remaining rigidly the same, but by her *metamorphosis* at the moment of her encounter" (Copjec 1999, 258). In order to persevere in Agirre's bertso song Lujanbio had to go through a thorough metamorphosis of her gendered and subjective personae. She became "the man" among the bertsolariak by bringing to the fore the radical need of a new female subjectivity for their song to preserve relevance for future generations.

The bertso song per se does not have to be a fight or a joko or a jolas or any other behavior but itself in principle. It does not have to be used for competition or cooperation; it does not have to be individualistic or communal. It may have aspects of any of those performative models, but in itself it is just a song. If Beckett stated in his *Texts for Nothing* that, "writing has nothing more to assert"(Badiou 2008, 263), so does a bertso have nothing to assert beyond itself. The song's true potency derives from being a song with no other purpose but itself. When two bertsolariak are singing facing an audience, there is a give and take between the two of them,[1] a sort of competition as to who will outwit the other, but it is a competition in which the public will like best the one who combines true verbal skill with the ability to crack logical or discursive orders in order to humor her companion and the public, as well as engage in self-mockery.

So what type of victory or failure is appropriate to the bertsolaria? As an artist, the bertso singer is always confronting an abyss of risk and ultimately faces some form of failure. But regarding *failure*, Beckett believed that it was the inevitable result of all attempts at artistic creation: "to be an artist is to fail as no other dare fail," and to retreat from failure was a "desertion." His conclusion was that the artist should make of "this admission, this fidelity to failure, a new occasion, a new term of relation," something that it could turn into "an expressive act, even if only in itself, of its impossibility, of its obligation" (Beckett, quoted in Cronin 1997, 572). Beckett would surely agree that what Zizek wrote about musical composers applies to writers as well: "failure is a sign that the composer is dealing with the *Real* of musical matter. It is only the 'light' *kitsch* composers who can pass from one smooth triumph to the next" (Zizek 2012, 604n45). A bertsolaria, likewise, each time she sings is confronted with failure—like Sisyphus up the slope. Failure is simply intrinsic to his/her song, as she could always have found a better wording, rhyme, tone.

In a championship, in which the value of a bertso is numerically measured and, vis-à-vis the audience, is conditioned by its proximity

---

1   There used to be a tradition among French Basque sheepherders to sing *txikitoak:* when two of them got mad they would start singing outrageous bertso at each other until they both broke down in laughter and thus the enmity ended; there was an element of "competition" in this tradition as well, not with the goal of winning over the other but of making yourself the greater fool and thus preventing a fight.

to winning, no such failure is considered intrinsic to bertso singing. In a competitively measured performance, the value of a bertso becomes "objective" and is determined not on the basis of its own poetic "nothingness," but on the value granted to it by a jury. The problem with such a competitive status of the bertso is that it has to measure as well the formal negatives that defy any measurement and which we will discuss in the next section.

Belief in the logic of success is of course central to the workings of the capitalist system that rules our lives. The consumer of commodities has to believe that these will provide the desired satisfaction. But, much like the excess that haunts desire, capitalism suffers from the crisis provoked by a surplus of production—none of it able to provide the ultimate satisfaction. Psychoanalysts tells us that while we consciously try to win, the subject's satisfaction in losing remains unconscious. In this view, the unconscious "impels the subject to act in ways that subvert its own interests, and the subject finds satisfaction in these acts because they produce a lost object for the subject to desire and enjoy. The subject's satisfaction is inextricable from self-destructive loss" (McGowan 2016, 15). In short, Freud looks at "loss as constitutive of subjectivity" and to the satisfaction the subject finds in repeating loss since "the subject's satisfaction is inextricable from failure" (Ibid., 28). Sarasua's self-sabotage or the preference shown by some bertsolariak for not winning are instances of such preference for failure.

The national championship is presented every four years as a spectacular success story that gives new life to bertso singing and therefore to Euskara as well. There are obvious benefits to such massive attention by the media, thus turning bertsolaritza into a fashionable art and creating new fans for such a highly formal skill in Euskara; a notable plus is that new young people become known to the public and thus become part of the bertso singing circuit and perhaps just this factor is enough to justify the championship. And yet, from a purely theoretical standpoint, one should keep asking to what extent such blunt application of the logic of success replicates the capitalist fantasy of the satisfying object.

Karen Horney identifies capitalism with competition and "the neurotic personality of our time": "From its economic center competition radiates into all other activities and permeates love, social relations and play. Therefore competition is a problem for everyone in our culture, and it is not at all surprising to find it an unfailing center of neurotic conflicts" (Quoted in McGowan 2016, 133). The bertsolariak themselves are the first ones to complain about the neurotization/ hysterization they have to endure during the season of competitive championships. It is perhaps the role of the feminist bertsolariak to recognize these deceptive trends in their trade and produce a radical reinterpretation that will allow the public to recognize where the true satisfactions of the art of bertso singing reside—in its constitutive lacks and failures.

Obviously, such an embrace of art's failure is the last thing the audience at a bertso championship wants to see. The public wants competition and the declaration of a winner. Deep down, the bertsolaria knows that her bertso could be improved in various ways, that it never reaches the perfection she aspires to. Nobody wants to be declared a loser, but one should not be surprised that a possible reaction among the winning bertsolariak is that they feel a hystericized unease regarding the fact that one's victory makes the others losers in a performance that is essentially verbal play.

In short, as in all art, new categories of analysis and new orientations of thought in bertsolaritza go hand in hand with new subjectivation processes in which the frontiers between the subject who knows and the song that she sings disappear.[2] As underlined by the feminist criticism of representation, the bertsolaria has to keep awareness of the extent to which cultural images are situated and interpreted within the context of patriarchal ideologies and competitive strategies external to the art itself. Since the bertsolaria's mental process is one of "argument of images" (See Fernandez 1986) the formation of a new imagery, grounded on the local experience of gender and cultural changes, as well as that on the political realities

---

2   For a parallel feminist approach to art production in the Basque context, see Zilbeti (2016, 11–20).

of the emerging global space, is critical to the recreation of the
bertso art and the formation of new bertsolaria subjects.

The Work of Theory:
From Lekuona to Lacan

In a recent book on Basque feminist art, Maider Zilbeti (2016) em-
phasizes the interlinked domains of the body experience, knowledge,
and theory in the formation of new subjectivation processes, subjects
who are at once inside and outside gender ideologies. Zilbeti's book
argues against the premise that sex should not be a category in the
production of art. She shows in particular the singular relevance of
theory in the development of critical feminist practices in art. In a
parallel manner the study of gender in relation to bertsolaritza brings
us face to face with the inaugural role of theory in its development,
as illustrated by the classical contribution made by Lekuona in 1935.

Lekuona's fundamental insight was that a bertso relationship
"is not one of idea to idea, but rather one of image to image"
(Lekuona 1935, 82; emphasis added) and he went on to incisively
describe the internal logic of such movement of images as charac-
terized by: 1. Abundance of *elisions* and "pregnant" constructions;
2. Linked by the *absence* of rhetorical-grammatical means; 3. *Careless*
logical-chronological order in the narrative succession; and 4. *Lack*
of logical cohesion between the images and the theme of the song.
This is all about the formal structure internal to a bertso and adds
no theory on issues such as gender and discourse and society. Still,
these pioneering ideas by Lekuona on the formally *negative* or *sub-
tractive* nature of bertso singing are pivotal in bringing bertsolaritza
to an up-to-date theoretical ground. What he is trying to theorize
is the gap the bertsolaria pierces in the grammatical, rhetorical, and
rational fabric of language—a smashing crack in its literal meaning
by the mere sound of homonymy and rhyme, a rupture or *nothing*
by which new images and new meanings are possible.

Thought, fantasy, emotion, and body—it is all tangled in a bertso
improvisation. The tone of the voice, the facial emotion, the gesture

of the body, the modulation of the melody will determine how the audience receives the gap of nothingness that a bertso conveys. As Hegelian philosophers endlessly discuss, is that "weird Something which is *less* than Nothing" (Zizek 2012, 304). Hit by the emotion and wonder of the moment, the audience has only applause to recognize the impact of that "crack" of the "something else" they have heard—before returning again to the abysmal silence and nothingness from which it all began.

Lekuona's discovery was that, by exploding relations of grammar, logic, rhetoric, chronology, lexicon, the art of the bertsolaria relies entirely on *subtraction*—the key operation by which truth can emerge out of language's excess. What we could add today to his theory is the preeminence that subtraction holds in contemporary thought. As Badiou has it, subtraction "is the act *par excellence*, the act of truth, one by which I come to know the only thing that one may ever know in the element of the real, and that is the void of being as such" (Badiou 2008, 113).

Badiou also examines Mallarme's poetic method through a multiplicity of subtractive operations and types of negation such as vanishing, cancelling, and foreclosure (Ibid., 49). But even in the poetry of the beat generation one can find a similar method of cancellations, as when Allen Ginsberg (2017, 388–89) writes about his own theory of poetry:

> the visionary aspect of poetry is when you present one clear picture and then without any explanation jump to another completely clear picture. The gap or space in between those pictures is a kind of mind space or gap in time or a gap in consciousness or a gap in vision. As in movies, the poignancy or charge or visionary aspect or satori or sunyata or mental electric comes from setting up one pole of thought from or word or picture and then setting up another pole. Then the mind has to fill in the space between by connecting them. The connection that the mind makes is like an electric charge between the two poles. The thought rises naturally in order to connect the two polarized images, disparate images, perhaps even opposite images, perhaps even contradictory images.

The bertsolaria's improvisation begins by the *elimination* of time, followed by the vanishing of grammar, logical argument, chronological order. Lekuona also used electrical metaphors when he described the ending point of the bertso "as if it were the bomb of the piece" (Lekuona 1935, 54). The bertsolaria is Mallarme's oral counterpart—every word, line, rhyme, and bertso a throw of the dice. In the cracks between the images, something actually has taken place through the song's cancellations and vanishing points—a moment of truth.

But it is regarding feminism that the theorization of bertsolaritza can be greatly enriched beyond Lekuona. His fragmentary view of the bertsolari text and his logic of subtraction lends themselves to contemporary elaborations of feminine subjectivity. As pointed out earlier, male fantasy loves to totalize Woman. Psychoanalytic thinking on sexuality starts with the insistence that it is "the locus of a fundamental *split,*" while something else gets added to the signifying order, something which is parasitic on performance and is not a being, but "it is discernible only as a (disruptive) effect within the symbolic field, its disturbance, its bias," something that magnetizes this field and produces "the dimension that Lacan calls the Real, which is related to the points of structural impossibility/ contradiction of symbolic reality itself" (Zupancic 2017, 40–41). The obvious conclusion from such thinking, one that is seminal for any rethinking of the role of sexuality in bertsolaritza, is that "the symbolic field, or the field of the Other, is never neutral (or structured by pure differentiality), but conflictual, asymmetrical, 'not-all,' ridden with a fundamental antagonism . . . [but] antagonism as such never simply exists *between* conflicting parties; it is the very structuring principle of this conflict, and of the elements involved in it" (Ibid., 41).

Lekuona's conclusion that a bertso relationship "is not one of idea to idea," and that the internal logic of the song's movement of images is characterized by elision, the absence of rhetorical-grammatical links, disorganized narrative cohesion, and lack of logical cohesion points to an overarching formal matrix: the *non-relationship* (in strictly conceptual, grammatical, logical, and narrative terms). And yet it is this "non-relationship" on which the entire song relies—a song that is capable of a deep subjective impact on the imagination, emotion, and sheer enjoyment of a large bertso audience, a song that conveys knowledge and satisfaction to the listener by breaking down the linear signifying structure of language, by a signifying lack that registers and echoes with the Freudian unconscious.

For the sake of this chapter's argument, such a "non-relationship" internal to a bertso song evokes a formal parallelism in psychoanalytic thinking regarding sex and the famous enigmatic Lacanian motto that "there's no such thing as a sexual relationship." This does not refer to sexual practices (the absurdity that people do not have sex), but the "lack" or "impossibility" refers of such a relationship refers rather to the philosophical/transcendental conditions of what Lacan calls "sexuation" in the manner that "man" as a signifier fails to represent a subject for "woman" as signifier, both sides involving intrinsically different modes of access to jouissance.[3] So one has to add immediately that "non-relation is not simply an absence of relation, but is itself a real, even the Real. What does this mean? . . . The lack of sexual relation is real in the sense that, as lack or negativity, it is built into *what is there*, determining its logic and structure in an important way" (Ibid., 18).

In his elaboration of the inconsistencies of sexual difference, Lacan developed his "formulae of sexuation" by which masculinity is defined by the universal function (always needs a constitutive exception), while the feminine is defined by the "not-all" (the set is non-totalized, thus needs no exception). Among the bertsolariak the universal position has been male of course, while women have been the exception—a status that is now undergoing radical change. A

---

3   The psychoanalytic explanation of such difference hinges on the above-mentioned notion of "castration" that affects women as well as men—basically, the alienation from our bodies produced by language that provides access to a larger symbolic order—but distinguished as female and male modes of castration, modes that "are asymmetrical and incommensurable with each other, not reciprocal and complementary, hence no direct relationship between them is possible . . . sexual positions [that] have nothing to do with biological gender; a woman can inhabit a male body and a man can just as easily inhabit the body of a female" (Reinhard 2017, xii). Another way to understand Lacan's saying is that the male/female difference cannot be written or formalized.

long philosophical tradition that goes back to the Greeks and Kant, and more recently elaborated by contemporary philosophy, states that "being is not-all, being itself never forms a totality. . . There is no whole of being, no 'all there is,' there are only appearances in their particularity" (Copjec 2003, 4). The result of this position is that the real ends up displacing transcendence. Lacan linked his theory of the "feminine" subjective position as "not-all" with the notion of infinity.[4]

The bertsolaria's endless improvisation is intimately linked to the twin notions of "not-all" and "infinity." In a bertso song each "point," each image, each strophe, each reply is a fragment in a potentially endless chain of metaphoric extensions, verbal rhymes, opposing stands, discursive cracks ad infinitum. The infinity of the linguistic situation allows for endless combinations in each bertso—which is why a bertso should never be repeated, the first and last time of each improvisation a reminder that the song is end-less, as well as why the formal limits of the melody and the rhyme are primary conditions for the singer to submerge herself in the endlessness of the linguistic possibilities. As such, bertso creation displays therefore the "feminine" logic of the "not-all." The cuts, inconsistencies, dissonances, ambiguities internal to each bertso strophe are complemented by the imagination and experience of the listener who is thus made participant in the event of each song.

It has to be underlined at the outset that "masculine" and "femi-nine" are not substantive gendered realities nor are they trapped in any binary logic; rather, they involve two subjective modalities. In psychoanalytic thought "sex is above all a *concept* that formulates a

---

4   "When I say that woman is not-whole and that that is why I cannot say Woman, it is precisely because I raise the question of jouissance that . . . is in the realm of the infinite"(Lacan 1999, 103). The modern idea of infinity has nothing to do with spiritualism; in contemporary thought there is a "another articulation of the finite and infinite," a sort of conceptual reversal by which, if traditionally "infinity" was the realm of idealist spiritualism, "today, the main argument for spiritualism, against radical materialism, relies on the irreducibility of human finitude . . . while it is today's forms of radical scientific materialism which keep the spirit of infinity alive" (Badiou 2005, 155). Noteworthy about the current psychoanalytic thinking is that the logical issues underlying its basic categories—"all," "exception," "not-whole," "castration"—are closely linked to such modern mathematical articulations of the finite and the infinite.

persisting contradiction of reality" (Zupancic 2017, 3)—not an ultimate reality but a persistent stumbling block in it. We could say that the masculine or feminine modalities are results. It is on the basis of an encounter and of the active or passive positions one takes.

Enjoyment is related to the gap in the signifying chain, a constitutive negativity whose name is sexuality, the placeholder for the missing signifier. What is thus "the real" of sex? It is not a simple ontological category but depends on "something which is not of the order of being, and which Lacan refers to as *the Real*. The Real is precisely not being, but its inherent impasse" (Ibid., 22). Badiou elaborates on this definition of "the real" as *absence* or the impossibility of a relationship—absence of sense which is quite different from the opposite of sense, or "nonsense": "Ab-sence, the name of the Real as opposed to ontology, is connected with the impasses of logic (the sexual relationship can't be written) and with (the being [*l'etre* of) the letter [*lettre*] as pure wordplay . . . ab-sence is located right within the relationship between performance and signifier" (Badiou 2017, 39).

And we might add: what is "the real" of a bertso if not such "absence" of sense and "pure worldplay"? Is it not something that belongs to the ontology of the signifying chain but is a crack in the grammatical and logical being that is present as lack, elision, antagonism, impasse. Yet such a "non-relation," either in sex or a bertso, is not an obstacle to creating a successful relationship or a successful bertso, but just the opposite, for it is the logic inherent to a bertso or to a sexual relationship. Following Lekuona's early theorization, we insisted on the *subtractive* quality of bertso formation—the gaps by which the bertsolaria pierces a hole in language's grammatical and narrative logic, the lack of rational sense by which the song becomes pregnant with metaphors, meanings, and emotions. Here is Badiou writing on the intersection of psychoanalysis and philosophy: "[Lacan's argument] is not an assertion of the nonsense of the real. Rather, it is an assertion that an access to the real can be opened only if it is assumed that the real is like an absence in sense, an ab-sense, or a subtraction of, or from, sense. Everything hinges on the distinction between ab-sense and non-sense."

Absence as subtraction of sense leads Badiou to "the formula" by which, including sexual relations, "*any function of the real in knowledge concerns, in positive terms, absence*" (Ibid., 50, 51).

Freud observed that there is no regard for contradictions in the unconscious. And so is the bertso indifferent to contradiction—as the argument of the song will deliberately seek contradictory words and images, ambiguity and paradox, to create a pun or suggest an analogy. Philosopher Barbara Cassin (2017, 7) establishes a "switching" between the Aristotelian logic's aporia of ultimate foundation, the principle of all principles that was "there's no such thing as contradiction," and the logic of Lacan's psychoanalytic formula that "there's no such thing as a sexual relationship"—a switch that conforms to the disregard for the principle of contradiction by the Freudian unconscious. The Aristotelian foundation of no-contradiction is based on the univocity of sense=essence, whereas the Lacanian foundation, like the bertsolaria's, is based on homonymy and equivocation and absence. Strict consonantal rhyme, based on the homophony of homonymous and polysemous words, is the most salient formal trait of bertso formation—it is, in short, anything but univocity. What is written about Lacan's "switch" applies to the bertsolaria: "the sole sense, the one-sense, is un-sense, that is, the deprived-of-sense (homophony always already enacts equivocation), or rather: it is signification, but not sense. There is no sense other than equivocation, and this is called 'ab-sense,' an escape from the Aristotelian norm of sense" (Ibid., 9).

How can the theorist formulate this world of primordial body experiences, imaginative fantasies, and formal absences? Faced with the difficulties of formalizing his understanding of sexual relationships, Lacan elaborated his criptic mathemes as a formal solution to the impasse of formalization—in order to transmit knowledge that "seems impossible to be taught" (Roudinesco 1997, 360). Similarly, what the bertso provides is a formal solution (by means or melody, rhythm, rhyme) to the impasse of formalizing such a massive transfer of verbal, imaginary, and emotional content toward the bertsolaria from the fans. The bertsolaria is faced with "the impossible" of improvising a perfectly settled bertso—it could always be changed, added, improved. She has only a few seconds to begin; her song is the only formal solution. Such impossible is "the real" in the Lacanian sense—what can never be fully symbolized or spoken, only sung by chance.

As the song on Xalbador by the poet Xabier Lete has it, "the deepest bertso, the strongest cry of the truths that can never be told." Truth holds onto the Real by such impossibility—a Real that at the limit of discourse will hit the bertso fans in their guts, making them laugh and cry, forcing them to lay their heads down in agonizing silence or raise up from their seats in raucous screams. A conventional view of artistic sublimation is that it is a substitute for sexual satisfaction; but Lacan thought that we can get from talking or writing or singing the same satisfaction, the point being not its sexual origin but that the satisfaction is itself sexualized. For the bertso singers and listeners, the song is itself not an object of sublimation but deeply embodied beyond its feminine or masculine contents.

Drinking and commensality are traditionally the most typical contexts for listening to the bertsolariak. In a real sense, the Basque equivalent of the ancient Greek institution of the *symposium* (a drinking together accompanied by conversation, music, song, and dance) is bertso singing during fiestas and banquets in which the most bodily and most imaginary realms of verbal and emotional experience are intermingled. Plato turned his classic text *Symposium* into the most celebrated treatise on love in the Western canon and Lacan interpreted it as the paradigmatic example of what psychoanalysts call *transference*. A deep relationship of transference identification from the bertso listeners toward the bertsolariak can be felt while the improvised song emerges slowly in a world of imaginative uncertainty and subjective desire. It would be easy to establish parallels between the position Plato ascribed to Socrates in his treatise and the one the bertsolaria holds for his communal audience. Socrates is the sage who never wrote, who knew and did not know what he was asked about; above all, he was the man who had the *agalma*, which is related to "sparkle," "charm," "uncanny," "god's trap" (See Lacan 2015, 141–43). Young beautiful Alcibiades was attracted to the old ugly master because he thought that "inside

Socrates lies a treasure, an indefinable, precious object which will fix his resolve after having unleashed his desire" (Ibid., 152). And yet Socrates refused Alcibiades's advances because to him "there is nothing in him that is lovable. His essence is . . . emptiness or hollowness" (Ibid., 154).

The bertsolaria is also endowed with the enigmatic agalma by which he or she is admired and loved, the owner of an uncanny treasure that will sparkle and satisfy the audience's desire. In Lacan's interpretation, "Love can, in effect, only be articulated around lack, owing to the fact that love can but lack what it desires" (Ibid., 124). The bertso art's very formal structure (based on ellipsis, lack, conceptual gaps, absent grammar) is a formal replica of the subjective desire's world of lack. In his or her song the bertsolaria provides a voice (hollow in its formal emptiness, pregnant with emotional and bodily content) to the very logic of desire—while it creates the satisfaction of its imaginary fulfillment and the jouissance of its transferential love.

A feminist perspective on gender relations goes against the grain of the allegedly harmonious perspective between the sexes in traditional societies, including notions such as Basque matriarchy, in which women need to fill very specific social roles. What is most exceptional about the role of women is precisely bringing difference to such cultural unanimity—the division as such that is intrinsic to social antagonisms, including sexual difference, characterized by lack and an ontological negativity that eschews the traditional essentialisms around the categories of "masculinity" and "femininity." In short, we are forced to think "not the contradiction between 'opposite' sexes, but the contradiction inherent to both, 'barring' them both from within" (Zupancic 2017, 72).

In the psychoanalytic perspective espoused here, ultimately sexuality ceases to be a cultural, moral, or identity issue to become an epistemological and political one (Ibid., 36). The relevance of contemporary feminism for bertsolaritza springs not only from contesting the exclusion of women, but even more from its capacity to insert into the allegedly neutral homogeneity of the bertso formations the gender differences that are key for understanding and transforming the current political situation. Sexuality is such a problematic territory because of its paradoxical ontological status, leading to limit concepts such as the feminine "not-all" and other complicated theses. The task of feminism in bertsolaritza is presenting sexual difference as a dimension of social antagonism, as ontological split within the symbolic homogeneity of the traditional order anchored on the domains of the masculine and feminine spheres, public and private spaces, and so on, an order which has resulted in massive subordination and exclusion for women—that is, feminism not as a reaffirmation of female identity but as a political problem of emancipation that affects all, women and men.

Bibliography

Astiz, Iñigo. 2013. "Iturritik oholtzarako malda." *Berria,* March 19.

Badiou, Alain. 2003. *On Beckett.* Edited by Nina Power and Alberto Toscano. Manchester: Clinamen Press.

———. 2005. *Being and Event.* Translated by Oliver Feltham. New York: Continuum.

———. 2008. *Conditions.* Translated by Steven Corcoran. New York: Continuum.

———. 2017. "Formulas of 'L'Étourdit.'" In Alain Badiou and Barbara Cassin, *There's No Such Thing as a Sexual Relationship: Two Lessons on Lacan.* Introduction by Kenneth Reinhard. Translated by Susan Spitzer and Kenneth Reinhard. New York: Columbia University Press.

Badiou, Alain, and Barbara Cassin. *There's No Such Thing as a Sexual Relationship: Two Lessons on Lacan.* Introduction by Kenneth Reinhard. Translated by Susan Spitzer and Kenneth Reinhard. New York: Columbia University Press.

Bateson, Gregory. 1972. *Steps to an Ecology of Mind.* New York: Ballantine Books.

Beckett, Samuel. 1976. *I Can't Go on, I will Go on: A Selection from Samuel Beckett's Work*. Edited and introduced by Richard W. Seaver. New York: Grove Press.

Camus, Albert. 1955; 1991. *The Myth of Sisyphus and Other Essays*. Translated from the French by Justin O'Brien. New York: Vintage International.

Cassin, Barbara. 2017. "Ab-sense, or Lacan from A to D." In Alain Badiou and Barbara Cassin, *There's No Such Thing as a Sexual Relationship: Two Lessons on Lacan*. Introduction by Kenneth Reinhard. Translated by Susan Spitzer and Kenneth Reinhard. New York: Columbia University Press.

Copjec, Joan. 1999. "The Tomb of Perseverance." In *Giving Ground: The Politics of Propinquity*, edited by Joan Copjec and Michael Sorkin. London: Verso.

———. 2003. *Imagine There Is No Woman: Ethics and Sublimation*. Cambridge: MIT Press.

Cronin, Anthony. 1997. *Samuel Beckett: The Last Modernist*. New York: Da Capo Press.

Fernandez, James W. 1986. *Persuasions and Performances: The Play of Tropes in Culture*. Bloomington: Indiana University Press.

Garmendia, Elixabete. 1987. *Yoyes desde su ventana*. Pamplona: Garrasi.

Ginsberg, Allen. 2017. *The Best Minds of My Generation: A Literary History of the Beats*. Edited by Bill Morgan, with a Foreword by Anne Waldman. New York: Grove Press.

Hernández, Jone M. 2018. "¿Acaso tiene género la sangre? O por qué los cuerpos femeninos no sirven como habitáculo para los versos." In *Etnografías feministas: Una mirada al siglo XXI desde la antropología vasca*, edited by Mari Luz Esteban and Jone M. Hernández García. Barcelona: Ediciones Bellaterra.

Lacan, Jacques. 1999. *On Feminine Sexuality: The Limits of Love and Knowledge*. Edited by Jacques-Alain Miller. New York: W.W. Norton & Company.

————. 2015. *Transference: The Seminar of Jacques Lacan.* Book 8. Cambridge: Polity.

Larrañaga, Karmen. 1995. "Andra bertsolarien historia." *Bertsolari* 17: 17–20.

Lekuona, Manuel de. 1935. *Literatura oral vasca.* San Sebastián: Kardaberaz.

MacCannell, Juliet Flower. 1994. "Things to Come: A Hysteric's Guide to the Future Female Subject." In *Supposing the Subject,* edited by Joan Copiec. London: Verso.

McGowan, Todd. 2016. *Capitalism and Desire: The Psychic Cost of Free Markets.* New York: Columbia University Press.

Olaizola, Manuel. 1976. *Sasoia joan da gero.* Tolosa: Auspoa.

Oteiza, Jorge. 1963. *Quousque tandem…! Ensayo de interpretación estética del alma vasca.* Zarautz: Auñamendi.

Power, Nina, and Alberto Toscano. 2003. "'Think, Pig!' An Introduction to Badiou's Beckett." In Alain Badiou, *On Beckett,* edited by Nina Power and Alberto Toscano. Manchester: Clinamen Press.

Reinhard, Kenneth. 2017. "Introduction to Alain Badiou and Barbara Cassin, *There's No Such Thing as a Sexual Relationship: Two Lessons on Lacan.*" In Alain Badiou and Barbara Cassin, *There's No Such Thing as a Sexual Relationship: Two Lessons on Lacan.* Introduction by Kenneth Reinhard. Translated by Susan Spitzer and Kenneth Reinhard. New York: Columbia University Press.

Roudinesco, Elisabeth. 1997. *Jacques Lacan.* Translated by Barbara Bray. New York: Columbia University Press.

Zilbeti, Maider. 2016. *Arte ekoizpen feministak euskal testuinguru kulturalean: Arte-instituzio garaikideetako pratika. Arteleku Zentroa eta Montehermoso Kulturgunea.* Bilbo: Udako Euskal Unibertsitatea.

Zizek, Slavoj. 1999. "There Is No Sexual Relationship." In *The Zizek Reader,* edited by Elizabeth Wright and Edmond Wright. Oxford: Blackwell Publishers.

————. 2000. *The Fragile Absolute.* London: Verso.

————. 2006. *How to Read Lacan.* London: Granta Books.

————. 2012. *Less than Nothing: Hegel and the Shadow of Dialectical Materialism.* London: Verso.

————. 2017. *The Incontinence of the Void: Economico-Philosophical Spandrels.* Cambridge, MA: The MIT Press.

Zupancic, Alenka. 2017. *What Is Sex?* Cambridge, MA: The MIT Press.

Zulaika, Joseba. 1985. *Bertsolariaren jokoa eta jolasa.* Donostia: Baroja.

———. 2014. *That Old Bilbao Moon: The Passion and Resurrection of a City.* Reno: Center for Basque Studies.

CHAPTER 7

Basque and Buckaroo: Women at Work in the Nevada Desert

Carolyn Dufurrena

"I see now that where I came wholly into the presence of the Land, there was a third thing came into being, the sum of what passed between me and the Land which has not, perhaps never could, come into being with anyone else."

Mary Austin, *The Flock*.

It seems that as we become close to the land, through working and living in the vast space with so few other humans, we become somehow different, more than the sum of our parts. I have spent three decades collecting the stories of women who live in this desert. It is in a way the story of my neighborhood, though the women lived here at different times and in far-flung valleys. Some are Basque,

some not, but they all have this in common: that they lived close
to the land, and the land made their lives rich with the experiences
they had there.

Mary Austin led a solitary life, married to a shiftless husband
who was seldom present, and mother to a daughter who suffered
from what we would probably call today severe autism. The daughter
was eventually institutionalized. Mary lived in a series of hamlets
along the eastern front of the Sierra Nevada on the California-
Nevada border from the late 1800s through the 1920s. During this
time, massive herds of sheep traversed what was called the Long
Trail from the valleys of southern California to the Nevada deserts.
Mary walked with the sheep as they came past her home near Lone
Pine. She befriended the herders, Basque, French, Portuguese, and
Chinese. She learned their stories, listened to their improvisational
songs and wrote them down.

"The great trunk of the trail," she writes in 1906, "begins in
Southern California, near Mohave . . . It lies along the east slope
of the Sierra Nevadas, and hugs the foot of the great Sierra fault
for a hundred miles through the knife-cut valleys, trending no far-
ther desertward than the scant fling of winter rains." (Austin 1906;
2001, 73).

> Herders, before undertaking the desert drive, turn into
> the alfalfa fields around Lone Pine. Here while the flock
> fattens they make camps of ten or a dozen; in the long
> twilights they sing and romp boyishly with the dogs,
> and here the wineskin goes about . . . when a company
> of Basque herders are met about the fire, in the whole of
> a long evening the wineskin does not touch the ground
> . . . There you will hear roundels and old ballades, and
> perhaps a new one (ibid., 67).

Mary Austin spent many hours in solitude in the desert, and was never
lonely in it. The landscape became a character in her narrative. The
mountains sustained her, and in the stories of other women of the
Nevada desert, it is evident that the landscape plays a part as well.

It was 1920. Rabies swept the remote high desert Antelope Ranch near McDermitt, Nevada, and five-year-old Juanita Yraguen, with her brother Fanneo and her sister Mary, had been sent to bring the cows into the yard. Fanneo, age seven, had a pitchfork. "I don't know how Mama would send us, all on foot, to bring those cows in" (Dufurrena 2010, 10–11). A rabid coyote had been in the herd, and Fanneo vowed to kill him.

"We were out there, and that coyote came right toward us. Fanneo shook his pitchfork, but then he said, 'Goddamn, I can't kill that coyote,' dropped the pitchfork, and ran for the house." Juanita and Mary stood, staring at the coyote. 'He froze and looked at us, and then he turned and went for the cattle.' It's a wonder he didn't get all three of them" (ibid.).

Juanita's parents had immigrated from the village of Ereño in Gipuzkoa to that dirt-floored stone house in Malheur County, Oregon. "Mama had the Steens Mountain to look at every day," Juanita told me in 2010. "She always said she would never have made it if she didn't have her mountain" (ibid.).

The decimation of their cattle by rabies and other economic factors caused the family to move the next year to Vale, Oregon, where they ranched for the next fifteen years, and where Juanita and her seven siblings learned English. She loved school and was good at math and sports, but it was the rule that the children would go to work after eighth grade. Juanita went to work as a nanny, cook, and chore girl for neighboring ranches for the next three years.

As as many Basque girls did, she met her first husband at the local Echanis Basque Boarding House, in Ontario, where her sister Timotea worked. She married John Ybarzabal in 1933. They moved home to her parents' ranch for a while, and built a herd of milk cows. She was eighteen.

Juanita would outlive two husbands and six of her seven siblings. She would build successful businesses, a restaurant, and be part of the group that founded the Basque Club in Ontario. When she died in 2013, age ninety-eight, she left four daughters, many grandchildren and great-grandchildren, and was a great-great grandmother of two.

Basque rancher and sheepman Alex "Buster" Dufurrena used to say that when you started horses, a young horse should be used almost to the limit of his endurance: not with cruelty, but with toughness. The harsh experience "makes them strong," he would say. "They'll be able to take a lot more later on." Perhaps this is the same with us. Juanita had a childhood as tough as anyone could imagine, but her life was long and rich with success, with friends and family.

Another young woman, Dale DeLong, moved as a bride from Golconda, Nevada, in 1934, to a remote ranch in the desert at the foot of the Jackson Mountains. This place is bordered by steep, black mountains to the east, and to the west by the playa of the Black Rock Desert, a stretch of ninety miles of greasewood and alkali, where nothing grows. She birthed her first child in a line camp shack on the gravel road to town. There would be three more children in the next years. She lived a hardscrabble, difficult existence in the most austere of circumstances, noting that there was "sand in the stew" many nights in buckaroo camp. She broke her back twice, the second time alone on the ranch in the horse corral, yet she loved her life and only unwillingly in her late eighties consented to move to assisted living.

In the 1950s, the Navy had a bombing range on the Black Rock Desert that bordered her ranch, and some days their target practicing went off course. This poem came from a story she told (Dufurrena 2016, 36–37).

"Four Silk Shirts" (1955)
She raised four kids on a lonely place
on the edge of the Black Rock Desert.
They lived on what they could raise or shoot,
ninety gravel miles from town.

She patched their jeans and mended
torn leather, reworked their duds again and again,
hoping for new things one day.

She slept on a bedstead tucked into the corn
when the ears came close to ripen.
Her rifle slept beside her underneath the summer moon.
She laughed when the deer heard the bedstead squeak:
They would give her plenty of room.

The fighter plane comes low and fast, practicing for war.
She starts as shells whack against the barn.
She sees the surprise on the pilot's face,
at the little family in the yard.

He's not much older than the boys,
she thinks, wondering where they are.
They'll come home late gathering strays that day,
down the desert, not so far.

Another day she hears him come, further off this time
looks up to see a mass of white,
fluttering to the ground.

She catches up the sorrel mare,
trots out to investigate,
a sheet of silk is captured there, billowing in the breeze.
She hobbles Sorrely some distance off
to save the long walk home.

Picking the fabric free of thorns,
She sees it's tattered, but not so worn,
so she rolls it tight,
ties it on and turns for home.

Heading back across the flat, colors come to mind:
mint green, sky blue, sun's yellow gold,
as it lights the baby's ear:
bright, soft pink as she's laughing there.

That night she cuts out four silk shirts.
It's almost time for Fair;
mint green, sky blue, sun's yellow gold,
bright pink of the baby's ear.

Beautiful, but tough and sleek,
they won't tear on barb wire or brush:
a second skin for her four young babes
riding the desert, far beyond her reach.

This woman lived without neighbors; her nearest in-laws were twenty miles distant. She raised her children with her husband, but did the work of the house and the range without female companionship. She lived to be ninety.

In another valley not too far distant, by local standards, from Dale's place, but nearly a hundred miles from town, was a family whose experience was very different. Three Basque brothers, their wives, their children, and their widowed mother all lived in one great house in King's River Valley. The eldest granddaughter, Ann Darlene Bengoa Jones, now eight, remembers: "I was born in 1938. My parents, Ann and Frank, ran what was then called the Commercial Hotel and restaurant in McDermitt. When I was about four," she recalls, "we all moved to the Kings River Ranch."

The house had been built in the old Basque way, by Tom Dufurrena, who owned the place from approximately 1936 until 1942. There was the big kitchen downstairs; then the dining room and the front room, three little bedrooms downstairs and a bathroom, and three big bedrooms upstairs and a little room. "That little room was my bedroom at first," Ann says, "but as the families got bigger, one bathroom wasn't going to work, so I moved into one of the upstairs bedrooms." They made a bathroom out of her room.

The wives rotated cooking duties. "The ladies who weren't cooking helped clean up, but still one person was in charge, so that was a long day for her. 6:00 breakfast, dinner at noon, and 6:00 supper. If it was just the family, it was nineteen or twenty people." Frequently the table included a couple of hired hands.

"My grandmother set the table," she says, "and you know those big long tables, they had these big heavy tan plates. She would deal those plates out like cards. They were heavy as could be, and she would get these plates and toss them across the table and they would land right there, where they were supposed to, so she didn't have to walk around"

"She always peeled the potatoes. That was her job in the morning, to peel all those potatoes. We made our own chorizos, we butchered all our own meat, pigs and a few sheep. We made our own cheese. It was a self-sufficient outfit. It was a lot of work, but everybody helped. And they all stuck it out, nobody left."

"There was no such thing as privacy, really," she says.

"You learned to keep your mouth shut, otherwise you'd never survive. Most people did too. There was an understanding. You can't live together like that and express your opinion. But every evening after dinner, the guys would sit in the front room and visit, smoke cigars, drink whiskey, and pass gas. It annoyed the ladies, but there was really nowhere else to go. Everybody was just trying to make a living, and they were long days. People were too tired to fight" (Jones 2017).

Though the traditional culture was solidly in place in this remote ranching environment, roles began to change with the end of the World War II. The ladies of the previous generation were occupied with the duties of the house, but Ann loved to be on horseback, and she was encouraged to buckaroo.

"I did ride all the time, but nothing like the younger kids did. I do remember being on horseback when I was about ten, taking the horses up Log Cabin Creek." Buckaroos would move the ranch cavvy up the mountain before branding; there were some eighty head of saddle horses and ten buckaroos. On this day, Ann Darlene was in the middle of it. "Well, something spooked my brown horse and he ran away. By the time they got him stopped I had run right into the middle of the horses, there were cowboys and horses going every which way." She did not, however, fall off.

"She was good help, damned good help," said one of the neighbor boys who rode with her. "She was just like her dad, Frank. His horse would be running full steam ahead down the hill and he'd be a-hollering; she didn't yell, but she was just as fast."

She demurs. "I don't think I was that much of a buckaroo compared to Ceci and Chris and Cleto," she says. She mostly worked the outside, holding rodeer with the rest of the kids, keeping the herd together. "I would just pray for a calf to break out so I could do something," she says.

Ann Darlene was the eldest of the fifteen cousins, who were reared as siblings. Born in 1938, at the end of the Depression and the beginning of World War II, her experience was vastly different than the younger children. There was no school in the valley until several years later, so Ann boarded with an aunt in Winnemucca during the school year from the time she was six years old. There were no more children born until the end of the war; she was basically an only child. The world became a much different place after the war.

"My sister Delphine was born in 1945, my cousin Ceci in 1947. Her brothers, Chris and Cleto, came along a year later. They went to school out there at the ranch."

Ceci Bengoa Ratliff is now seventy, and lives on a ranch in Moses Lake, Washington. "We were kind of like the Three Musketeers," she says, of her exploits with her twin brothers. They spent as much time as they could outside. "I was probably three when I learned to ride," she says. "I had a big paint horse; he was so big I looked like a fly up there."

"Mom home-schooled us through my third grade year," she says. She did her kindergarten lessons, finger painted, and learned to read by the stove in the big ranch kitchen. Later, Old Chris, her dad, fixed a space in the building across from the big house. "We actually had a little schoolroom there, and my mom was the teacher. Dad would go across and build a fire in the winter, and write us little notes on the blackboard. We did that until the end of third grade, when there were two more school-age cousins, Frank and Margarita, and more kids in the valley. Then they set up a schoolhouse on the ranch for the whole valley. I went there until I was in eighth grade. Then Mom and Dad bought a house in town" (Ratliff 2017).

Traditional women's work conflicted with their heart's desires, and both girls learned early that they could be part of the big world outside the ranch house.

"I always liked to be outside and ride," says Ceci. "I did that as early as I could, and as much as Dad would let me." She tells about having trouble with a zipper on a sewing project. Ceci's mind was always out in the corral, this day "because they were roping and branding horses." Her mother finally said, "Go; get out there." She knew it was a futile task at that moment to keep her daughter's mind on sewing.

"There's a picture of me in a little yellow dress when I was about three, 'helping' my dad, or getting in his way, out in the blacksmith shop. I had so much soot on that yellow dress, it was more black than yellow by the time I got done," she says.

Ceci's paint horse ran away with her when she was just three; actually, he ran home from the meadow outside the gate. "I was pretty scared," she says, "but it didn't keep me from going again. Dad was pretty protective of his little girl. He would let the boys, a year younger than me, go along on longer rides than I at a younger age. I did not think that was quite right," she says, "but then I grew into it, and I was one of the cowboy crew. I was probably nine or ten when I was able to go ride and gather in the canyons."

Both girls would work the hay crew when they were a little older, fourteen or so. They learned to drive a rake in the new age of mechanization, when one swather took the place of six men cutting hay with a six-foot sickle. They spent their summers through high school between the hay fields and the mountains with the cattle.

"We didn't have an opportunity to work anywhere but the ranch," Ceci says, "since we were eighty or more miles from town. I used to think I wanted to get a job at the café in Orovada, but Dad didn't like that idea. I would have used up all my wages in gas. I loved working on the ranch, in any case. I guess I could have helped in the house more, cooking and that, but that's not really what I wanted to do." She laughs.

Ceci was part of a generation that had greater opportunities to do what they wanted. Although they lived in a remote valley, in a traditional world, these third generation Basque-American girls had an essentially American experience, an expanded opportunity to discover who they might be in the world of work.

By 1979, women were being incorporated into many aspects of traditional men's employment. As a field exploration geologist working for a multinational mining firm, the author encountered this Basque family, doing the work of the ranch in the tradition of neighboring. There was no prejudice toward women working in the male world. The work was the important thing, the only thing.

"In my first year in the country, as they say here, I was working in the red rhyolite above the Bengoas' place, looking for minerals for a Colorado exploration company" (Dufurrena 2002, 20). Tim was working for another ranch down the valley. I guess you'd say we were courting, when courting involves only the work that each of you does, black sky above the steam of hot springs at night, a campfire in the wilderness. No dining, no dancing, no movies. He helped me take water samples, crack rocks looking for mineralization. I showed him country he hadn't seen before. Turnabout is only fair play. "Want to come with me tomorrow?" he asked, when I overheard the conversation he was having with someone on the telephone. 'I'm going to help Bengoas.'"

I could ride, sort of. A seventh-grade summer at camp, a few trail rides in Colorado on family vacations. They put me on a gentle, ugly horse. Old Chris, the cowboss, had smiled at me, the city girl one of his cowboys had snagged in passing.

(I have to wonder now, if Old Chris was thinking of his buckaroo daughter Ceci, grown now and married to a rancher far away.)

We all sat on our horses in the yard, waiting to go. I took off my jean jacket, deciding I wouldn't need it, and dropped it across my saddle horn, unsure what to do with it. The horse, startled, huffed, humped up, took a crow hop. I had no idea what to do. I looked straight ahead, and found Tim's eyes looking straight back at me. He wasn't laughing at me, or condescending. "Drop the jacket," he suggested quietly. So I did. The old horse settled under me. Somebody got down, took the jacket, hung it on a post. Nobody laughed at me, at least right then. They gave me the benefit of the doubt; I saved face by not falling off. Then--nothing. No teasing, no bullshit, nothing. We just turned and left the yard, weaving through willow-fringed meadows behind a mass of cattle.

Tim rode a runaway brown colt that kept bolting; he would bring him back, get him settled. Then a rabbit would jump up from the brush, the colt would panic again, and off they would go, Tim's pressed white shirt barely visible in a cloud of dust. The horse I was passenger on knew what he was supposed to do: he followed the cows. I admired the scenery.

We could barely see the desert windmill that was our destination when a storm blew through, driving a cold, late-fall rain into our faces. Chris gave me his old hat; a pair of ancient leather gloves, stiff as wood. It felt good to pull them on over my frozen red hands. Later his wife, Mary, brought us lunch, thick sandwiches and hot coffee. In the back of her truck he found a square of green irrigating canvas and a bit of twine. He slit the canvas part way up the middle, and poked holes for the twine with the point of his branding knife, fashioning a pair of chaps. Tied the whole awkward arrangement around me. It was not pretty, but it was a lot warmer out of the wind.

"Do you want to go back to the house?" Chris offered. "You can ride back in the truck, and we'll bring the horse."

Not me, not for a second. Tim was not saying anything. He was driving cows.

At the end of the drive, they brought the trailer, and we bumped back up the long valley in the cold rain of darkening afternoon. Shivering, wet to the bone, I followed the men through the living room into the big, high-ceilinged kitchen. Yellow light warmed dark wood walls and overstuffed leather armchairs polished by years of use. An impossibly long, linoleum-topped table was set with heavy ceramic plates, thick white mugs, great bowls of food. Glass-paned cabinets held stacks of white dishes, heavy glass tumblers. The aroma of freshly made coffee, chile rellenos, and stew was intoxicating.

Standing in the kitchen, the men passed a half-gallon bottle of Early Times, one slug apiece, to warm up. Chris jokingly offered it to me. Shaking from the cold, my plaid shirt still damp, I took it. He laughed like hell, but it was fine with him if I were one of the boys; we all needed to get warm. Tim stood off to one side, watching me, smiling a little behind his big black beard.

I can't say, even now, if that day wasn't bait. Willingly taken, to be sure. I loved the cold in the morning, the smell of horses and leather, wet jeans and dust, the meadow-hay sweetness of cattle kept in outside country, their quiet energy as they moved along, the low rolling clouds bringing rain--all of it. I loved all of it, that day.

They let me be who I was, and go along, and if I learned something or liked it, that was okay. There was a space held there for me; I could just be.

The day was an invitation, like putting a salt lick in a clearing and backing off to see what the deer will do. Here's the life, what do you think? Quiet, focused, waiting for me to make the choice. Nobody had ever put me in that place before.

There was a deep privacy acknowledged. In this kitchen, there were things going on that weren't spoken conversation, subtext that was all eyebrow and smile, but that communicated acceptance nonetheless.

One clamped hand loosened that day on the desert around my idea of who I was and what I would become.

I could feel this thing tugging at me. What could I be in this world? Still, something in that quiet, focused waiting, the accepting silence, recognized what I knew needed acknowledgment: he saw through the cleverness and urban polish into something I barely recognized about myself, something that surfaced that stormy November afternoon.

I valued independence above all things; yet the loneliness that is freedom's partner was eating away inside me. I needed the vast, empty spaces to range through, and the warm, yellow hearth at its center.

The ranching culture, the Basque culture, was a loose net thrown lightly over a whole mountain range. The people described it as "our mountain, our territory, our way of life. These Basque families were like groves of aspen trees, individuals to the naked eye, but connected at the roots, all one organism.

The culture valued work above all else, and whether one was man or woman did not seem, by the late 1970s, to make much difference. If one put in the work, with energy and dedication and hopefully a measure of expertise, the respect garnered was the same.

The land supported, and still supports, those who work in solitude in the desert landscape, male or female. Where one comes wholly into "the presence of the Land," there is indeed a third thing which comes into being. Man or woman, but especially woman, I believe as Mary Austin did that, "we become greater than the sum of what passes between us and the Land." Once in that presence, the things about which we write become more than the sum of our experience, as well.

Bibliography

Austin, Mary. 1906; 2001. *The Flock.* Afterword by Barney Nelson. Reno: University of Nevada Press.

———. 1932. *Earth Horizon: Autobiography.* New York: The Literary Guild.

Bengoa, Mary, and Lisa Ratliff Scott. 2002. "Bengoa Family Tree." Unpublished manuscript.

Bidart, Grace. 1996. "Oral History by Linda Dufurrena." Humboldt County Library Oral History Project, Winnemucca, NV.

Bidart, Grace. 2017. Interview with author, tape recorded.

Dufurrena, Carolyn. 2002. *Sharing Fencelines: Three Friends Write from Nevada's Sagebrush Corner.* Salt Lake City, UT: University of Utah Press.

———. 2010. "Juanita Yraguen Ybarzabal Hoff: Still dancing after all these years." *Range Magazine* (Winter): 9–11.

————. 2011. "Rosemary's Story." *Range Magazine* (Winter): 72.

————. 2016. *Quiet, Except for the Wind: Poems and Stories from the Cold Desert.* Denio, NV: Quinn River Press.

Echeverria, Jeronima. 1997. *"Eskaldun Andreak:* Basque Women as Hard Workers, *Hoteleras,* and Matriarchs." In *Writing the Range: Race Class and Culture in the Women's West,* edited by Elizabeth Jameson and Susan Armitage, Susan. Norman, OK: University of Oklahoma Press.

Etchart, Marianne Yribarne. 1996. "Oral History by Linda Dufurrena." Humboldt County Library Oral History Project, Winnemucca, NV.

Jones, Ann Darlene Bengoa. 2017. Interview with author, tape-recorded, Winnemucca, NV.

Goldaraz, Mary. 2018. Interview with author, tape-recorded, Winnemucca, NV, January 17.

Goldaraz, Resu. 2018. Interview with author, tape-recorded, January 12.

Lowry, Rosemary Obieta. 2011. Interview with author, Jordan Valley, OR.

Ratliff, Cecelia Bengoa. 2018. Interview with author, tape-recorded, January 22.

Stevens, Marge Dufurrena. 1994. "Oral History by Linda Dufurrena." Humboldt County Library Oral History Project, Winnemucca, NV.

Thursby, Jacqueline. 1999. *Mother's Table, Father's Chair: Cultural Narratives of Basque American Women.* Logan, UT: Utah State University Press.

CHAPTER 8

Work Song:
A Female Voice from Cow Camp

Amy Hale Auker

Livestock Man (slam poem)

I need to write a new poem about what it is like, as a woman, to cowboy for a living.

But all I can come up with is how much I hate it when my toes get cold.

All I can think about is that last old cow we put on the trailer for the sale barn, about the scorpion that ran away when I rolled my bed out on the ground at Alkali Spring in August, about how I alone can catch that roan mare when she won't let the men lay a hand on her.

All I can come up with is how much I like cows, and like them, I have ovulated, copulated, gestated a miracle in my body, and lactated ... for months.

I think I'm qualified to be a herder of mammals.

And that is what I am. I am a herder, a custodian, a caretaker, a steward.

I am a livestock man.

I grow food.

I need to write a new poem about what it is like, as a woman, to cowboy.

But there are no new poems and we're never finished shipping cattle in the fall.

There may be new foxes in the night and new orioles in the canyon and new griefs to be borne and new ways of looking at the world... Oh, please, don't let me become blind.

And I might become blind if you put me in the cage of your expectations.

For I have a rebel heart, and that rebel heart gives me the grit to stay in my saddle even after it turns sideways when the bullfight breaks and we're in the way.

And that rebel heart says this poem ... doesn't have to rhyme.

I need the language to tell about what it is that I do, but all I have are nouns:

weather and wind and wool,

rock and rattle and remuda.

Smoke and sweat and sunrise and savvy.

Tracks and trails, tinajas and tally.

Cow and count and coffee and canyon,

logistics and latigos and loops.

Moonshadow, mud, mother, manure, moisture in the air.

Hooves and javelina and how sharp is your pocket knife?

I need the words to tell this story but all I have are verbs:

pee in the dirt

and dally up and build again

and don't cry when you get yelled at.

Back off that little heifer and ride up! Don't let that bull bluff you out. We'll never get him again.

Thaw the frozen coffee pot.

Blink the smoke out of your eyes.

Wipe the blood off your chin.

Dig the snowballs out of your horse's hooves.

Hurry up and get the gate; there's a storm moving in.

Open a can of chili. Let's eat before it gets plumb dark.

I need to write a poem about working for $75 a day, but all I can think about is that last little cow we left behind up on the mesa.

We'd been gathering into the trap for four days and our first calf heifers run in the general herd and our bulls are out year 'round. She gave birth overnight but she didn't bring her newborn in to hay ...and we had to go.

We cut her back with that ol' hooky cow's daughter and her calf because that ol' hooky cow's daughter is mean, meaner than that ol' hooky cow ever thought about being,

...and no lion or coyote is going to get that baby.

But then it snowed.

And I don't know what it is you think about when you lie awake at night...

Do you ever think of soft tender hooves and fresh new life up under a cedar tree at 6000 feet with a mama who's new to this gig?

I need to write a new poem about what it is like to cowboy,

Without the requisite body parts.

Wanna see my tattoos?

I do not like cut flowers. Perhaps because I am one who loves roots, fine hairy tendrils that cling and anchor, fat white tubers that nourish greenness above the soil. Perhaps it is because I cherish wholeness and connectedness, the potential for reproduction, rather than ovaries chopped from plants and wrapped in plastic, colorful petals that wilt and fade and fall, to be swept away into our compost.

Sixty or seventy mornings out of the year, I wake up in a canvas and wool bedroll, having spent the night on the ground. Very often, we wake surrounded by horses and cows, waiting to be fed. And while the division of labor in cow camp sometimes falls along traditional lines, it is more because of practical consideration than gender or subjugation. I am not mechanically inclined, and the men have more upper body strength. I can't out-muscle anything. Over the course of the last decade though, I have come to realize that if I substitute brain and well-placed leverage for physical brawn I can get just about any job done. On these mornings at camp, when the men disappear into the gloom and cold of early dawn to start reluctant motors or lug heavy bales, I move toward the previous night's ashed-over coals and begin my own work.

During my senior year in high school, I took the standardized aptitude test developed by the United States Military. The Air Force began calling our home asking if I had ever considered training to be a logistics officer. I had scored very high on that section of the test. Only after my father intercepted one of the calls and informed the recruiting officer that I am under five feet tall did they give up. Skills in logistics make for a very good camp cook though, no matter my height. Besides, when the coffee pot is not frozen solid, I like building a fire, frying bacon in cast iron, settling the grounds with cold water when the coffee finally boils. I like outfitting for camp, planning food for six or seven days ahead, layering the meals and meats in the cooler. And I like watching our mama cows come down out of the trap, gathering around the hay that the men have thrown out, my hands wrapped warm around coffee in a tin cup. The men come to the fire I have built to eat, to get warm, to watch with me as the cows chew hay. Very soon, we will saddle up and ride, the traditional job of cowboy now genderless.

I come to this place, not as an academic studying a culture or a question, but as a worker, as a ranch hand, as an observer, with hours and hours to study, in depth, this act of growing food by managing a herd of ungulates in rough country where things grow up out of the ground, where other beings graze, and all life sways within the weather and seasons where we must dwell in harmony with thousands of diverse species. I come to this place as a woman. I come to this place as a poet. It is in this place I find my voice. And I am not the only one.

In her book *If Women Rose Rooted: The Journey to Authenticity and Belonging*, Sharon Blackie (2016, 12) writes, "The world which men have made isn't working. Something needs to change. In order to change the world, we women need first to change ourselves—and then we need to change the stories we tell about who we are." As much as I admire Blackie and her writing and the strong premise of this book, I believe she has this statement backward. When we go to the land where we were once rooted and grounded, the work and the land will tell us who we are. The earth will show us the way, and we will regain, rewrite, re-find, and refine, our stories and our voices. We will have new songs, new stories, new speaking grounded in the ancient, yes, but rising into the daylight of who we are and what we have now. We will be changed. And the world will be changed. It is not that we change and then go out to do the work. It is that we work, no matter our place or calling, and we are changed. This is how it has been for me.

Ovaries outnumber testicles on a cow drive, by a lot. The shouts of men and roar of machines are drowned here, by space and distance and sweeter songs, the mating songs sung by the males of other species, the song of water and plants straining toward the sky, the song of mothers calling to offspring, the song of hooves and pads on the ground. I found my voice here in this work. At first, when I was slow to get the cows out of the gate and on the trail, causing the herd to be gapped and lagging, with the potential for disarray, my husband, an experienced cattleman, told me, "Sometimes you have to get a little mad." That is not part of my nature. To be angry when working with animals seems out of place. So, I do not get angry. I get mad. I become a crazy woman, yelling at the placid stragglers until they move out of the gate in good time, until they get the message, and we line out on the trail together. And then I can allow that energy, that madness, to sink back to a mother rhythm. Yes, I have learned to be boss. And I have learned to put my horse behind the final cow in line, one of the herd, one of the community. In time, I have learned to be graceful with a rope. I have learned to see when a cow has been sucked and might have left her calf behind, napping under a bush, out of sight. I have learned to read the stories in the dirt on the trail in front of me: where walked the coyote, the fox, the elk, the cows, the bear, the lizard with heavy tail. I have learned a soft song of "shhhht shhhtttt shhttt" mimicking a rattlesnake, the venomous natural sound that keeps everyone moving along. I came, early on, to appreciate the long, boring, quiet cow drives when no one needs to make much of a sound, because we all move in energetic accord.

Women—all women—are equipped to be herders of mammals and planters of seeds. After all, like these cows, we are mothers. We are grandmothers. We are aunts. We are daughters. We are lovers. We are sisters. We nod at that cow (or ewe or sow) with big belly, softening vulva, and tightening bag. She may give birth tonight or next week, but either way, I know this walk we are taking to the next pasture will do her good. We all must be fit in order to give birth to babies, to ideas, to poems, to songs, to sisterhood.

And this work on the land requires that we sing a holistic song. The word holistic is about seeing all of the pieces of something, but only as they relate to the whole. We must see not only that one plant, the one holding the soil of the creek bank, but also the bull bellowing down the way, eating the tops out of the ash seedlings. I must consider the approaching clouds and the month and the distance from here to camp. I must note each cow's udder, whether her offspring is following her, and then, I must take note of the tracks on the trails, the species of that bird in the bushes, and sidestep the gopher snake moving uphill. She is telling me that the approaching clouds are serious. And my husband, as foreman, must consider me, not only as wife and lover, but employee, and the man riding next to him, not only as friend, but name on the company payroll, and personality, and horseman. We consider the horses between our thighs as full on-partners, personalities, members of our team. If we are wise, we are aware of each nail in each iron shoe; we ride in rough country. We note where the remnants of ancient camps lie scattered on the ground, for those who came before us not only lived where the water was reliable season by season, but the evidence of their lives anchors us in the bigger history of this place. They left us messages; if we could only read. Like them, we consider the availability of water, the terrain, and the movement of the animals. Today, we also take into account the mechanics of the machines we use and the practicalities of human-placed dates on the calendar. If the season for hunting deer with rifles opens next week, we consider getting as many cows as possible moved this week, before the forest is full of hunters. We consider our neighbors, our fence lines, and those who will someday eat this beef that we are tending. We consider our impact on budgets, creek banks, schedules, and if these cows look better or worse after they've spent time with us. My husband constantly considers our partnerships with government agencies, the markets, and the financial bottom line of the ranch owner. He considers his tone of voice as he yells across the drive, for we must crawl inside the same bedroll after sitting around a shared fire and meal and drink after we have stepped down and unsaddled tired horses. A holistic view means that the whole is greater than the sum of all parts, and tonight, that seems to be true.

And so, all this is a portrait of my work. And I consider that it is my voice. No longer is my voice derived from the day's tasks and the life I am living, but the work has become my voice, the only song I care to sing. If someone were to ask me what I care about the most, I would say cows, the natural world, and writing it all down. But I could also add reading and gathering. Because from this work of growing food, the culture of living on the land, herding production animals and cultivating plants so that others might be nourished, come so many beautiful and strong female voices. Blackie (ibid., 278) states, "Traditionally, women have always come together to plant seeds, gather herbs, cook soul food, share stories and make medicines, and to pass on their wisdom and knowledge. Women are the core of a healthy community, and also at the core of a healthy community and world is respect for women, their voices, their medicine and their work." I gather these voices around me, pull them from my shelves often, memorize pieces of these poems and carry them with me while I ride. I recite them from the stage when I leave the solitude and loneliness to gather with them in person. And, as Clarissa Pinkola Estés (1992, 15) points out in her introduction to *Women Who Run With the Wolves: Myths and Stories of the Wild Woman Archetype*, their "Stories are medicine."

Linda Hussa, in her book *Blood Sister, I Am to These Fields*, writes poems of such an intense intimacy that they defy genre and gender. In "Love Letters," she describes staying in bed while her lover lights the morning fire, *"a kept woman, a moment longer,"* because she knows that, *"within an hour's time, we'll be ahorseback in a long trot to some distant blue mountain hunting cows"* (Hussa 2001, 133). She will be working. In her poetry collection, *In the Company of Horses*, Virginia Bennett writes of the mountain lion, as much a part of her work as the cow. *"She has ample time to consider her options/Whether scientists believe she can reason or not"* (Bennett 2004, 57). And Sue Wallis writes of a cow that kept leaving the bunch: *"Like me she has a spiritual affinity for solitude/ For lotsa grass and running creeks and growing babies at her side…"* and in the end, Wallis concludes, *"Still, like me, she knows deep down inside/ That herds of any kind are dangerous/And far too unreliable/For trust"* (Wallis 1994, 61). Weather is a constant theme for those who live and work uninsulated from the sway of nature's moods. Deanna McCall, New Mexico rancher, is not insulated from the seasons, ever. In her poem, "I'll Ride Thru It," she writes of external weather, *"When the cold makes my bones ache, but there's work to be done/For those cows and calves sake, I'll finish what's begun./I'll ride thru it. . . . When dust sticks to my sweat, heat bouncing off the ground/Horse's shoulders dripping wet, no breeze is to be found/I'll ride thru it."* McCall goes on to bring us inward, shows us where she goes for solace: *"When struggling to understand life's peaks and falls/My soul seeks the range land, I answer her siren call/I'll ride thru it"* (McCall 2018, track 8). Perhaps one of the most poignant songs that come from the land is that of the unsung woman, the huge numbers of women who never wrote their lives onto the page. Award-winning poet, Patricia Frolander, includes in her book, *Married Into It*, a glimpse of those women, with her poem "Denial" (Frolander 2011, 32):

> *Our neighbor called it "his ranch,"*
> *yet each winter day found her beside him*
> *feeding hay to hungry cows.*
>
> *In summer heat,*
> *you would see her in the hayfield,*
> *cutting, raking, baling, stacking.*
>
> *In between she kept books,*
> *cooked, cleaned*
> *laundered, fed bum lambs.*
>
> *Garden rows straight,*
> *Canned jars of food*
> *Lined cellar walls.*
>
> *Then she died.*
> *I asked him how he would manage.*
> *"Just like I always have," he said.*

These voices are just a few examples. Bennett, Gaydell Collier, Linda Hasselstrom, Nancy Curtis, Jill Stanford, Teresa Jordan, and many other editors and scholars have gathered the words of rural women from the American West into collections that resound with work songs. These voices of women working at growing food with dirty fingernails, in line with an ancient goddess earth culture, these voices rising in the West from what was once considered a male profession, hence the word cowboy, are often soft, often strident, always strong.

Blackie (2016, 278) writes, "It seems that it's taken so little time to lose the rich knowledge that was built up over thousands of years by our ancestors in this land." She writes of Scotland, but appeals to women on the land everywhere, both transplanted and indigenous. The voices of the women in the West join in harmony with a global singing. As female voices continue to emerge and strengthen worldwide, the stories from women in agriculture, those growing seeds and herding livestock, may be some of the sweetest. This is not a statement supported by documentation and research so much as by our instinctual listening, as we strive to turn up the volume, that this music coming from a place of healing and story might be heard.

Do not bring me cut flowers, pieces of what might remain whole and complete and fertile. But rather, bring me seeds and soil, gift me with a flat of crooked-neck yellow squash seedlings. I will dig deep, and they will rise rooted just as the women of the land. These women with the weather in their voices, ropes tied on their saddles, shoulders pulled by buckets of water carried to stock, these women watching with sharp eyes and keen noses, singing a birthing song, will rise, will rise all over the land. And we might have to get a little mad.

Bibliography

Bennett, Virginia. 2004. *In the Company of Horses*. Paso Robles, CA: Timberline Press.

Blackie, Sharon. 2016. *If Women Rose Rooted: The Journey to Authenticity and Belonging*. Denmark: September Press.

Estés, Clarissa Pinkola, PhD. 1992. *Women Who Run with the Wolves: Myths and Stories of the Wild Woman Archetype*. New York: The Random House Publishing Group.

Frolander, Patricia. 2011. *Married Into It*. Glendo, WY: High Plains Press, 2011.

Hasselstrom, Linda M., Nancy Curtis, and Gaydell Collier, eds. 1997. *Leaning Into the Wind: Women Write from the Heart of the West*. New York: Houghton Mifflin.

Hussa, Linda. 2001. *Blood Sister, I Am To These Fields: New and Selected Poems*. Reno, NV: The Black Rock Press, University of Nevada, Reno.

Jordan, Teresa. 1992. *Cowgirls: Women of the American West*. Lincoln, NE: Bison Books, University of Nebraska Press.

McCall, Deanna. 2018. "I'll Ride Thru It." *I'll Ride Thru It*. CD. Tularosa, NM: Deanna McCall.

Smuts, Jan C. 1926. *Holism and Evolution*. New York: MacMillan, Compass; Viking Press.

Stanford, Jill Charlotte, ed. 2016. *She Speaks to Me: Western Women's View of the West through Poetry and Song*. Lanham, MD: Two Dot, registered imprint of Rowman & Littlefield.

Wallis, Sue. 1994. *Another Green Grass Lover: Selected Poem of Sue Wallis*. Lemon Cove, CA: Dry Crik Press.

Index

A

B

Z

Made in the USA
San Bernardino, CA
16 February 2020

64389218R00136

Conference Papers Series No. 15